EUROPEAN COMPETITION POLICY

EUROPEAN COMPETITION POLICY

Peter Montagnon

editor

PUBLISHED IN NORTH AMERICA FOR

THE ROYAL INSTITUTE OF INTERNATIONAL AFFAIRS

COUNCIL ON FOREIGN RELATIONS PRESS
• NEW YORK •

Chatham House Papers

General Series Editor: William Wallace
West European Programme Director: Helen Wallace

The Royal Institute of International Affairs, at Chatham House in London, has provided an impartial forum for discussion and debate on current international issues for 70 years. Its resident research fellows, specialized information resources, and range of publications, conferences, and meetings span the fields of international politics, economics, and security. The Institute is independent of government.

Chatham House Papers are short monographs on current policy problems which have been commissioned by the RIIA. In preparing the papers, authors are advised by a study group of experts convened by the RIIA, and publication of a paper indicates that the Institute regards it as an authoritative contribution to the public debate. The Institute does not, however, hold opinions of its own; the views expressed in this publication are the responsibility of the author.

Library of Congress Cataloguing-in-Publication Data

European competition policy / edited by Peter Montagnon.
    p.   cm.—(Chatham House papers)
    ISBN 0-87609-090-0 : $14.95
    1. Competition—Government policy—European Economic Community countries.   2. Industry and state—European Economic Community countries.   I. Montagnon, Peter, 1950–   . II. Series: Chatham House papers (Unnumbered)
HD3616.E833E96   1990
338.6'048'094—dc20
                       90–2352
                       CIP

90 91 92 93 94 95 96 PB 10 9 8 7 6 5 4 3 2 1

CONTENTS

FOREWORD

The full benefits of the single market will not be attained without an effective competition policy. Thanks to a succession of vigorous Commissioners, the European Community is now set on a course which will produce a genuine European competition policy in place of the present set of varied and uncertain national ones. But, like so much in the European Community, scaling one foothill serves only to reveal other and more difficult obstacles to surmount. This Chatham House Paper looks at some of the more important of these – merger policy, control of state aids, international competition and the largely uncharted terrain of regulation of the utilities on a Community scale. Peter Montagnon and his fellow authors have provided valuable pointers to the European competition policy of the future.

This study is one of several run by the West European Programme of the Royal Institute of International Affairs. The Institute acknowledges with grateful appreciation the support of the Gatsby Charitable Foundation, Courtaulds plc, the Department of Trade and Industry, the Eurotunnel Group and IBM (Europe) for the programme as a whole. Particular thanks are due to Mercury Communications Ltd and BAT Industries for sponsoring this study and associated work, and to Sir Leon Brittan and the staff of DGIV in the Commission of the European Communities for their help and encouragement.

July 1990   Michael Franklin
                              Chairman, West European Programme

ACKNOWLEDGMENTS

Many people in and out of government helped with the preparation of this study by attending study groups, by making themselves available for interviews, and by commenting on the draft text. I am grateful to all of those who gave so generously of their time. In particular I should like to mention my fellow authors, Heinrich Hölzler, Joseph Gilchrist and David Deacon, for their patience and courtesy during the editing process. At Chatham House itself, I am indebted to Sir Michael Franklin, Helen Wallace and Steven Woolcock for their wise counsel, as well as to Pauline Wickham and Hannah Doe for their work on the text. Finally, Dieter Helm of Oxford University provided some invaluable initial research for the chapter on regulating monopoly utilities.

July 1990   Peter Montagnon

1

INTRODUCTION

Peter Montagnon

'Competition policy – conducted at the Community level – would have to operate in such a way that access to markets would not be impeded and market functioning not distorted by the behaviour of private or public economic agents. Such policies would not only have to address conventional forms of restrictive practices and the abuse of dominant market positions, but would also have to deal with new aspects of anti-trust laws, especially in the field of merger and takeover activities. The use of government subsidies to assist particular industries should be strictly circumscribed because they distort competition and cause an inefficient use and allocation of scarce economic resources.'

This statement from the 1989 Delors report on economic and monetary union is typical of the importance now attached to competition policy by the European Commission in connection with the 1992 single-market programme. Starting with the Padoa-Schioppa report of 1987, and continuing with the Cecchini report published in the following year,[1] the Commission has developed the argument that Europe will reap the full benefit of the single market only if the opening of internal trade barriers is accompanied by the full and free play of competition. Anti-competitive policies, and the pursuit by member states of their own national industrial policies, would stand in the way of a

Community-wide restructuring and would deprive Europe of the efficiency gains it is seeking from the 1992 project. Cost benefits would be lost, and growth opportunities would disappear.

How Europe rises to this challenge will influence not only the success or failure of the single market in economic terms; it also has an important bearing on the future political shape of the Community. Because it is concerned with establishing a fair playing-field for business at a European level, policy towards competition is one of those areas in which the Commission may often be pitted against the sovereign will of member states; but if it is to implement a strong and coherent European policy in this area, it must assert its own independence and authority. There is little doubting the determination in this respect of Sir Leon Brittan, the responsible Commissioner. In practice, however, political realities may often dictate compromise. Where such compromise falls will help determine more generally the balance of power between Brussels and the individual member states. It is hard to imagine the European Community being anything more than a loose economic federation if weakness at the centre allows member states to continue in pursuit of their own narrow economic interests.

Of course, the need to achieve a competitive environment for the single market is not the Commission's only priority; a strong regional policy is also needed to bind the Community together. Without that, there is a risk that the poorer peripheral regions of Europe might feel disadvantaged as the economic gains appeared to go mostly to those central regions where wealth is already concentrated. Similarly, many have argued that attention needs to be focused on social policy. Workers displaced, or threatened with displacement by the adjustment process, are likely to become disillusioned with the European ideal unless their problems are addressed by social policy. The starting-point of this study, however, is the notion that the Commission has to take the lead in securing a competitive environment for 1992 and beyond.[2] If this is not a key objective, the economic success of the 1992 project would be jeopardized. Regional and social policy can smooth the development of the single market; on their own, however, they cannot bring about the benefits which Europe is seeking.

This raises questions, not only about the interaction between competition policy and other objectives, but also about how well the Commission is equipped, in terms both of legal powers and of manpower resources, to rise to the challenge. The Treaty of Rome, by which the European Community was founded, contains some strong language about competition, not only in Article 3, where general principles are enunciated, but particularly in its pivotal Articles 85 and 86 (see Appendix I). Article 85 prohibits practices and associations between undertakings or firms 'which may affect trade between Member States and which have as their object or effect the prevention, restriction or distortion of competition within the Common Market'. Article 86 prohibits 'any abuse by one or more undertakings of a dominant position within the common market or in a substantial part of it ... insofar as it may affect trade between member states'. The Commission has long used these Articles vigorously to combat the formation of cartels. Like his Irish predecessor, Mr Peter Sutherland, Sir Leon Brittan has taken a strong and proactive approach to other areas of competition policy. Often, however, such an approach depends on a particular interpretation of the rules. Future Commissioners may choose to strike a different balance between, for example, competition policy and industrial policy. Given the importance of competition to the success of the single market and the growing power of the Commission in this area, one of the main purposes of this study is to examine the degree to which the Commission is both able and obliged in practice to count the maintenance of competition as a leading priority.

It goes without saying that the development of the single market will require continued vigilance by the Commission against the formation of cartels. In this respect, however, there is not much change from what has gone before. This study focuses instead on four other areas. Although some of them lie outside the narrow traditional definition of competition policy, all of them have become what might be termed 'stress-points' for policy towards competition in Europe after 1992. They are: mergers and acquisitions, control of subsidies, the regulation of utilities, and the link between trade policy and competition.

The study finds that in most of these areas the Commission has considerable discretion, but it is facing a sharply increased workload. There are also weak spots in its legal armoury, as well as areas of potential conflict with other Community policies. Within Europe, moreover, there is still widespread disagreement on some key questions. Should policy concentrate just on competition or should other matters of public interest be allowed to override competition from time to time? If so, how is public interest to be defined, and who should define it? Is there a risk that competition policy might simply become an arm of a European industrial policy managed by the Commission? Are there adequate safeguards to prevent this?

The ultimate economic goal of the single market is to boost both output and living standards in Europe. Underlying this is the expectation that it will engender an industrial revival which would allow European business to catch up the ground it is perceived to have lost to competitors in the United States and Japan. Such a revival could not happen without a painful restructuring, however, in which some weaker companies would go to the wall, leaving the field open to their stronger competitors. Particularly in the newly liberalized sectors like air transport, telecommunications and financial services, firms will be under pressure as never before. More generally, European industry will no longer be able to hide at the national level behind preferential public procurement policies and technical standards designed to keep out imports. Some firms are bound to seek shelter from the storm by running to their governments in search of subsidies. Others may seek to manoeuvre themselves into a dominant position from which they can keep the competition at bay. This, for example, is the motive some have attributed to Air France's move in early 1990 to acquire UTA, the second French carrier. The merger would make it the controlling French carrier on almost all the air routes out of France, as well as the dominant line on domestic routes.

There is thus a delicate balance to be struck in the execution of policy towards competition. Although the formation of anti-competitive business concentrations would damage the single market, its benefits will not be realized without rationalization in some sectors. One task of competition policy is to distinguish between beneficial rationalization and harmful concentration. This paper starts and finishes with the contention that the Commission is most likely to succeed in doing so if its policy is focused precisely on competition questions and does not become distracted by other matters loosely described as being in the public interest.

It is also clear that this is a long-term task. The restructuring on which the revitalization of European industry depends is to be induced through the elimination of internal trade barriers. This will produce an intensification of competition which, many expect, will eventually see fewer and stronger firms in each sector producing more goods, more cheaply and for a larger market. Although other outcomes are also possible, as the concluding chapter notes, such a process could ultimately produce a situation in which there is less competition as weaker firms are swallowed up by their stronger rivals. In terms of the cost to consumers, there may not be much difference between having one European manufacturer of railway locomotives with a monopoly hold on the entire Community market and several separate companies, each with a monopoly in its own national market. It is very difficult to tell in advance at what point along the rationalization road the benefits stop and the danger zone for competition is reached. Here again, the best protection is constant vigilance on the part of authorities dedicated to preserve competition. This protection would be weakened if it were diluted by any preconceived notion of what sort of industry Europe needs and how it should be organized.

The main body of this paper begins with an examination of the situation regarding mergers and acquisitions (Chapter 2). With the new merger regulation agreed at the end of 1989, the Commission has finally achieved powers that it has been seeking for sixteen years. It will have the exclusive right to vet the largest mergers affecting the Community, and its power may increase further in four years time, when even medium-sized mergers are expected to come under its jurisdiction. Yet a closer look at the new regulation suggests that many basic issues remain largely unresolved. As it stands, the regulation will apply only to a small proportion of mergers within the Community; and there is still room for doubt about the degree to which competition is the only yardstick by which mergers should be assessed, or whether they could be approved on broader grounds of public interest. There is also considerable concern about whether the Commission is adequately staffed and properly organized to deal with the extra responsibility. For all these reasons, this chapter argues, it may be necessary to build on the regulation by creating a separate European authority in this area. This is a controversial suggestion at present, but one which may have to be considered in order to keep the emphasis on competition as the main criterion for merger control.

Chapter 3 deals with state aids, or government support for industry in its various forms. It argues that particular discipline will be needed in this area after 1992, since subsidies will be one of the few means left through which governments can protect their own national interests. Not only have state aids been growing rapidly in recent years; there is also a wide divergence in the degree to which member states make them available. Currently the Commission concentrates on the basic task of vetting new aid schemes proposed by member states to see whether they qualify for a derogation from the basic ban on such aids contained in Article 92 of the EEC Treaty. Too little time is spent examining existing schemes to see whether they distort trade and competition. As part of a radical change in the thrust of policy towards state aids, the Commission should adopt this criterion as its main yardstick. It should concentrate on aids to the largest 1,500 companies in the Community, since these receive the bulk of available aids and little is known about the cumulative effect on competition of the aids they receive through different schemes. This chapter stops short of proposing a blanket ban on state aids to large companies, but it suggests that strict controls should apply even to research-and-development aids, which it describes as the sacred cow of community policy. A differentiated approach to aids may be needed for regional policy reasons, it says, but regional policy objectives would be better served by curbing aid flows to the richer central regions of the Community than by permitting higher aid levels in the poorer peripheral regions. Budgetary constraints make it difficult for these poorer regions to find the resources to administer the relatively generous amounts that they are already permitted by Brussels.

In Chapter 4 discussion turns to the regulation of utilities such as telecommunications, gas, electricity and water. Regulation of these utilities is a particularly daunting task because to a greater or lesser degree all of them involve an element of natural monopoly. The Commission has worked hard to introduce competition into these sectors, but it depends heavily on the cooperation of member states, which is often conceded only grudgingly. In telecommunications it has managed to push through some reforms by the controversial use of Article 90, which subjects public-sector undertakings, or those, such as utilities, vested with special and exclusive rights, to the normal competition rules of the Treaty of

Rome. Its insistence on being able to use this Article to impose reform without consulting member states prompted several members, led by France, to challenge it in the European Court. If the Court rules that Article 90 cannot be used in this way, reform momentum in this area will slow. Although the Commission needs the cooperation of member states, it also needs the legal powers to coerce. Meanwhile, reform of the utilities poses some delicate regulatory questions. It is essential to ensure not only that new entrants retain access to an existing distribution system where necessary, but also that they are not penalized by the existence of standards which favour existing operators. Above all it may be necessary to tilt the playing-field in favour of new entrants initially, so that they can gain the critical mass which would give them an effective role. Ideally, special European regulatory bodies are needed for this. Member states are unlikely to agree to such a measure, however, and this will impose an extra burden on the Commission's competition authorities.

Finally, Chapter 5 looks at the links between trade policy and competition policy. Both are concerned with market access, but this chapter warns that a protectionist trade policy could work against competition by sheltering firms from world markets and reducing the pressure on them to adjust. Anti-dumping actions are often seen as the international arm of competition policy, but in fact there is evidence to suggest that there is a connection between such actions and the formation of cartels. Similarly, calls for reciprocal treatment by the authorities of third countries in matters relating to investment and public procurement could lead to measures that are counterproductive in competition policy terms. There is a need for the interests of competition and of consumers to be represented more forcefully when decisions are made concerning trade policy. Ideally Europe might consider creating an Industries Commission to ensure that trade policy takes account of competition and consumer interests along the lines of that which operates in Australia. At the very least its procedures should be changed so that Directorate General IV, which concentrates on competition policy, is formally consulted each time trade policy measures of a restrictive nature are under consideration. Its opinion about the effect of the decision on competition should be made public.

Notes

1 T. Padoa-Schioppa, *Efficiency, Stability and Equity: a Strategy for the Evolution of the Economic System of the European Community*, Report of a Study Group appointed by the Commission of the European Communities, Brussels, 1987. Paolo Cecchini, *The European Challenge, 1992: the Benefits of a Single Market*, Commission of the European Communities, Brussels, 1988.

2 The present study forms part of a series of wider projects being conducted by the West European Programme of the Royal Institute of International Affairs relating to the 1992 process. In particular, it is written in parallel with the forthcoming Chatham House Paper *The Changing Industrial Map of Western Europe* by Professor Aubrey Silberston.

2

MERGER CONTROL

Heinrich Hölzler

Despite their resolute attachment to the idea of free competition, the founding fathers of the European Economic Community saw no need for a specific merger control system. Article 3 of the EEC Treaty, which launched the Community in 1957, explicitly affirmed the need for a system of undistorted competition, but the Treaty makes no provision for merger control.

This seems puzzling at first glance. Not only did the Treaty of Paris, which had established the European Coal and Steel Community six years earlier in 1951, contain such a mechanism; it is nowadays almost unanimously recognized that a consistent framework of competition rules must include provisions, not just against cartels and abuse of market domination, but also against mergers and acquisitions which could create or strengthen such a dominating position. Yet, in the mid-1950s, coal and steel were considered a special case because of fears that market dominance in this area could be a springboard to rearmament. For the rest, none of the signatories to the EEC Treaty then applied any merger controls of their own. The need for such control at the Community level was thus simply not thought of as a matter of priority. As a result, the Treaty contains only two short rules applying to anti-competitive behaviour by enterprises. Article 85 outlaws horizontal and vertical agreements between enterprises which restrict competition, for example through price-fixing, market-sharing or transactions which discriminate against third parties. Article 86 bans firms from abusing a dominant position. The creation or strengthening of a dominant position as such is, however, not prohibited at all. With the passage of time it became clear that Article 86 was comparatively less important. In practice it was very difficult for the Commission to prove legally that a dominant position was being abused. Even the existence of a dominant position could be established in only a few cases.

In dealing with mergers, therefore, the Commission has so far had to rely mainly on the terms of these two Articles. It has sought to use them to develop a powerful competence in this area. Yet its awareness that Articles 85 and 86 provide only a flawed basis for such powers has at the same time led it into a long struggle for a more formal instrument. Shortly before Christmas 1989 it finally succeeded. On 21 December, the Council of Ministers agreed a new merger control regulation which is to come into force in September 1990 (see Appendix II).

This chapter examines the history of the European merger control debate and the significance of the new regulation. In its conclusion it warns that, partly because of limits to the administrative capacity of the Commission, the regulation may fail to deliver either the consistency of approach which much of European industry has been seeking, or the free competitive environment which ought to be its aim.

An early milestone in the Commission's efforts to make the rules of Articles 85 and 86 apply to mergers came with the celebrated Continental Can case of 1972.[1] In this case the Commission was seeking to block an attempt by the US firm Continental Can Co. to create, through acquisition, a dominant stake in the European canning industry.

The European Court of Justice ruled that Article 86 could in fact be used to block a merger that distorted competition if it created an enterprise so dominant in a particular market that there was no practical scope left for real competition. Considering that Article 85 banned restrictive practices by agreement between firms, the Court took the view that firms should not be allowed to merge and then behave in exactly the same way as if they had made a prohibited cartel agreement. Both Articles 85 and 86 sought to achieve the same objective, namely the maintenance of effective competition within the common market as prescribed in Articles 2 and 3 of the EEC Treaty. It would be wrong if something that were illegal under one Article should be permitted under another just because the circumstances were different. 'Such a diverse legal treatment would make a breach in the entire competition law, which could jeopardize the proper functioning of the common market.'

The admission of this principle by the Court seemed an important advance. In the early years of the Common Market the main policy concern relating to industry had been to strengthen it through restructuring. By the early 1970s, however, attention had shifted to merger control, and in 1973 the West German government became the first original member state to institute such a system at national level.* Two years earlier, on the basis of the so-called Berkhouwer report, the European Parliament had requested the Commission to introduce a notification system for mergers and acquisitions likely to involve a significant increase in market share of consolidated turnover. Wrongly, as it turned out, the Continental Can case seemed to lay the basis for establishing a merger control system at European level.

On 20 July 1973, the Commission presented its first draft proposal for a merger regulation to the Council of Ministers. The proposal was relatively simple, at least in comparison with the complex text agreed upon sixteen years later. It included the following main elements:

- The regulation should apply to corporate concentrations with a worldwide turnover of at least Ecu 1bn.
- Pre-merger notification was mandatory and the Commission was empowered to introduce a proceeding within three months.
- If the Commission did not open a proceeding, the concentration was deemed to be compatible with the Common Market. Otherwise a decision had to be taken within nine months.
- Concentrations which would enable the merged firms to impede effective competition within the EEC should be

*The United Kingdom, which joined the Community on 1 January 1973, the same day as Germany introduced its merger control regulation, had had its own instrument in this area since 1965.

declared incompatible with the Common Market, but an exemption could be granted if the concentration was needed to help achieve an overriding Community objective.

Hopes were high in the Commission that this regulation would be passed. The European Parliament, as well as the Economic and Social Council, approved it with a large majority in February 1974. Only minor amendments were proposed and the Council of Ministers was supposed to make its final decision by the end of that year. However, exploratory meetings showed that member states were not willing to agree to the transfer of sovereignty over industrial policy that the regulation would involve. Quite a number, including Italy, Britain and France, at that time wanted to retain national control over merger policy in order to further their own industrial policy objectives. Although the Commission continued to seek merger control powers, its task was made more difficult by the Court's reliance on Article 86 in passing judgment in the Continental Can case. The legal and evidential difficulties of proving the existence of a dominant position within the EC or a substantial part thereof, and particularly of showing the abuse of such a position, made Article 86 hard to apply as a merger control instrument. This also meant that the Commission had little leverage over member states in its effort to make them agree to a European-level regulation.

With the onset of a new wave of merger activity both in Europe and elsewhere in the mid-1980s (see Table 2.1), the Commission began to look more to Article 85 as an instrument for control. Although it had long before argued that Article 85 could not be applied to mergers,[2] the Commission found that the picture changed dramatically as a result of a ruling by the European Court in what is now seen as the pivotal Rothmans-Philip Morris case of 1987. The history of this case goes back to 1981 when Philip Morris acquired from South Africa's Rembrandt group half the equity in Rothmans Tobacco Holdings, which in turn had a majority holding in Rothmans International. The agreement provided for joint management of Rothmans and exploitation of benefits in joint distribution and manufacture. Following complaints by other cigarette companies the European Commission objected to the arrangement. A new deal was struck in which Philip Morris agreed to transfer back its shares in Rothmans Tobacco Holdings and take a direct 30.8 per cent stake in Rothmans International with its voting rights restricted to 24.9 per cent. Although the European Commission was satisfied with this arrangement, two companies, BAT and R.J. Reynolds pressed their objections in the European Court. In its judgment, the Court rejected their specific complaint but ruled that in principle the acquisition of a minority shareholding might constitute a violation of Article 85 under certain circumstances.[3]

Table 2.1 National, Community and international mergers in the Community (including acquisition of majority holdings)

	1983/4	1984/5	1985/6	1986/7	1987/8
National	101	146	145	211	214
Community	29	44	52	75	111
International	25	18	30	17	58
Total	155	208	227	303	383

Source: Commission of the European Communities, *Annual Reports on Competition Policy*.

This effectively meant that agreements on the acquisition of shares in competing enterprises might fall under Article 85 to the extent that they influence the market behaviour of the enterprises concerned and that competition between them was distorted or restricted. As far as the Commission was concerned this was tantamount to a form of merger control authority. In fact, the scope of the judgment remained legally and politically ill-defined, creating what many saw as an intolerable burden of uncertainty for industry. One argument ran, for example, that Article 85 could not be applied to acquisitions of majority shareholdings, since majority control of one enterprise by another eliminates the independence of the second firm, making illegal agreements between them impossible. However, not being able to rely with certainty on that argument, industry feared that Article 85 could be used retroactively, making a merger or the acquisition of a minority shareholding that had already taken place null and void, as well as any subsequent undertakings by the two companies. Private parties, as well as the Commission, could invoke Article 85 and institute proceedings against mergers. Even when the

Commission was prepared to use its powers to exempt a merger from being covered by Article 85, the exemption could last only for a limited period, usually not more than five to ten years. In the face of all this confusion and an increasingly activist approach on the part of the Commission under the then responsible Commissioner, Mr Peter Sutherland, industry itself began to press for a clearer set of rules. It was this as much as anything else that finally led to agreement on a new merger regulation.

This chapter has dwelt at some length on the history of the merger control debate in Europe because it is relevant to any assessment of the new regulation. On the one hand, it demonstrates the shortcomings of Articles 85 and 86. On the other, the failure of member states to agree earlier to a Europe-wide control system shows just how determined they were to cling to their own sovereign powers in this area. Indeed the basic questions before the Council of Ministers at the end of 1989 were the same as those of 1973. Should decisions be made exclusively on the basis of competition, or should other matters of public interest be admitted as a yardstick? And should the Commission have exclusive rights to determine whether a merger was admissible, or should member states also retain some form of control? Whatever the shortcomings of the merger control regulation, it was a remarkable achievement for the Commission to have orchestrated any form of consensus about these questions at all. Yet the fact that they had lain unanswered for so long also allowed the most extraordinarily diverse approaches to the problem to develop in different parts of the Community. The new regulation has had to take account of this, with the result that it is likely to be less than fully effective as a Community-wide merger control instrument.

Of all member states, Germany stands out as placing the strictest emphasis on competition as a yardstick in its regulations for assessing concentrations. The Federal Cartel Office takes a particularly strong line in this respect, although its procedures still allow for public interest to be taken into account. If the office prohibits a merger, the parties concerned may apply to have the decision set aside on public policy grounds by the Ministry of Economic Affairs. However, this exemption can be granted only after the Cartel Office has completed its inquiry and announced its decision. Since 1973 there have been only six such cases, the most recent being the Ministry's decision to permit the merger between the MBB aerospace concern and Daimler-Benz, to which the Cartel Office was opposed.

This system of exceptional and open exemptions from a strict competition yardstick puts Germany into a very different category from those member states that consider it essential for their governments to have immediate power to allow mergers where the overall economic advantages are perceived to outweigh any impediment to competition. In practice, the United Kingdom differs little from West Germany in its approach, but this is more the result of a conscious policy decision than the way in which the rules are formulated. Although competition is the main yardstick in practice, it would be perfectly possible in theory for the Secretary of State for Trade and Industry to ask the Mergers and Monopolies Commission to investigate a merger on grounds other than competition, and for the Commission to find that, although a merger had no particular implications for competition, it should be prohibited on the wider grounds of public interest.

Elsewhere, countries like France, Ireland, Portugal and Spain tend to place more emphasis on the non-competition aspects of public interest.

Add to this uneven approach the demand from industry for greater clarity in the legal environment and a 'one-stop shop' for merger authorization to replace the current diverse national responsibilities, and it is clear why a great deal of political momentum had built up behind the merger control debate. From the practical point of view there is an element of the absurd in the regulatory regime as it has existed until now. Under it, Siemens and GEC, for example, felt it necessary to refer their bid for Plessey separately to the British, German, French, and Italian governments, as well as to the EC Commission.[4] Yet the starting-point in the quest for a simpler approach is the diversity of system applied by individual member states.

Theoretically a harmonized approach to merger control within the EC could have been achieved by the alternative approach of changing national laws, but this would have been an even more complex process than the creation, through agreement by the Council of Ministers, of a 'one-stop shop' in Brussels. There is no doubt, however, that the European solution had to be a compromise in which member states with the largest distance from the centre had to concede most. Even so, the result is a compromise of doubtful validity. The decision to apply the regulation initially only to mergers between companies with an aggregate turnover of Ecu 5bn or more means that it cannot be effective as an instrument of Community-wide control. Ecu 5bn is quite simply too high to cover transactions involving most firms from smaller member states. There are niche industries, such as speciality pharmaceuticals, where the entire European market may be only a fraction of the threshold. Although such cases may still be dealt with by national authorities, and although their impact on the European economy as a whole may be small, the high threshold means that there will be differential approaches not only between individual member states but also between different industrial sectors.

Moreover, although member states are empowered to delegate their authority to the Commission, it is thought unlikely that many will in practice do so. Even small states like Denmark and Greece, which have no merger control regulations of their own, are unlikely voluntarily to place matters of potential public interest into the exclusive hands of the Commission.

Basic structure of the regulation
It is now time to examine the basic structure of the new regulation. There were three particularly contentious points in the discussions surrounding its preparation: the scope of its application, the degree to which public policy criteria as well as simple competition should be an admissible basis for judging mergers, and the relationship between the regulation and national competition laws. This section examines each of these issues in turn.

When it comes into force in September, the new regulation will apply to large mergers with a Community-wide dimension. These are defined as those in which the aggregate world-wide turnover of all the companies concerned exceeds Ecu 5bn and where the aggregate Community turnover of at least two of them is more than Ecu 250m.* The purpose of the Ecu 250m rule is to prevent broad application of the regulation to mergers taking place outside

---

*The Commission considers that the establishment of a turnover threshold will not prevent it examining cases such as Hoylake/BAT Industries, where Hoylake is a vehicle company with no turnover. The turnover of companies associated with it would be computed into the threshold.

the Community. If two US firms merge and only one has a large Community turnover, the regulation will not apply. An exemption from the turnover rules applies when each of the firms achieves more than two-thirds of its aggregate turnover within one and the same member state. This was designed to prevent mergers of basically national significance falling under Community competence.

The plan is that, after some experience has been gained in the operation of the regulation, these thresholds may be revised downwards. The regulation provides for them to be reviewed by the Council at the latest by the end of the fourth year following its entry into force. As part of the review, the Commission will propose new thresholds. After its discussion, the Council will vote on them on the basis of a qualified majority. A unanimous vote will not be needed. In theory this should make it easier for the thresholds to be reduced, thereby increasing the scope of the regulation. During the final round of discussions on the regulation, the United Kingdom sought to prevent this by insisting that the thresholds could be changed only by unanimous vote of all member states.

Reduction of the thresholds will none the less almost certainly involve another bitter argument. Even in real terms, the Ecu 5bn figure is substantially higher than that of Ecu 1bn originally proposed by the Commission in 1973. In setting this threshold, the Council took the view that the regulation should apply only to the most significant corporate concentrations in its introductory phase. Only with the later revision of the thresholds would the regulation be extended to cover most concentrations with a Community-wide dimension. Some countries, such as the United Kingdom, France or Germany, with well-developed anti-trust instruments of their own, may remain reluctant to transfer additional power in this field to the Commission. Proposals by the Commission automatically to reduce the thresholds after an initial period to Ecu 2bn – which is still a high figure – were emphatically rejected by the Council, as was the idea of introducing a lower threshold for turnover within the Community itself. There is therefore a risk that the agreed initial thresholds may remain in place for longer than the four years currently anticipated. For the foreseeable future, the regulation will therefore simply not apply at all to most European mergers, whether or not they have a Community-wide dimension.

The appraisal criteria under which mergers were to be judged had meanwhile been a critical issue right from the beginning of the discussion on the regulation. Indeed it was in this area that the ideological battle within the Community was the toughest. In the course of a protracted set of negotiations between the Commission and the member states numerous compromise proposals were advanced. All of them focused on the same question: should a merger be vetted purely on the basis of its effect on competition, or should other public policy criteria be taken into account? Not surprisingly, the answers showed variations from one state to another.

Early drafts of the regulation left the door wide open to consideration of public interest matters other than competition. The final text contains some explicit language, which is regarded, in the United Kingdom at least, as affirming the central position of competition. The key part of its Article 2 reads as follows:

> A concentration which does not create or strengthen a dominant position as a result of which effective competition would be significantly impeded in the common market or in a substantial part of it shall be declared compatible with the common market.
>
> A concentration which creates or strengthens a dominant position as a result of which effective competition would be significantly impeded in the common market or in a substantial part of it shall be declared incompatible with the common market.

Many of those involved in the negotiations on the merger regulation regard this as a satisfactory outcome to a long battle to establish competition as the yardstick by which mergers could be judged. These clauses appear to leave no room for the Commission to permit an anti-competitive merger because there is some other perceived public benefit to be gained. Equally they can be interpreted as depriving the Commission of the powers to block a merger just because it was perceived to be against the public interest.

Thus, for example, it would have been theoretically possible for the Commission to have barred the Nestlé bid for Rowntree in 1988 on the sole grounds of competition. By contrast, as noted above, the United Kingdom might have barred it on grounds of other public interest, although, of course, it did not choose to do so.

One view that can be taken of the regulation at this point is that it creates the scope for a European merger control system which is far less likely to be subject to political pressures from narrow vested interests than those which operate at national level. Certainly the current Commission gives every sign of intending to operate the regulation in this way. In that sense it will help enhance the competitive commercial environment within the Community. The question is, however, whether this interpretation of the regulation will be taken lying down by some of the powerful sectoral, national and industrial interests which may be affected. To take another theoretical case, one could ask how the United Kingdom would have reacted if the Commission had found that Kuwait's holding in British Petroleum could not be declared incompatible with the common market because it did not affect competition. Although the United Kingdom did order divestment on competition grounds, the debate was intertwined with national interest considerations. The assumption has to be that where these, or the interests of any major company, are under threat as a result of the regulation, no effort will be spared to push through a different interpretation of the rules.

Here the problem is that the regulation suffers from imprecision in its fine print, which leaves it open to a range of interpretations. It is not, for example, clear how the Commission is obliged to interpret the word 'significantly' in assessing any impediment to competition under the clauses cited above.

It is not surprising that a regulation negotiated between parties with such widely differing philosophies should be vulnerable to charges of ambiguity. Law-making requires precision which is almost impossible to achieve in a political negotiation such as that which gave birth to the regulation. Its final wording is a compromise designed to allow each government to justify the result achieved at home. Elsewhere in Article 2 this has led to a veritable pot pourri of possible factors that may be taken into account. These are set out in the two subsidiary paragraphs of Article 2(1), which read:

(a) the need to preserve and develop effective competition within the Common Market in view of, among other things, the

19

structure of all the markets concerned and the actual or potential competition from undertakings located either within or outside the Community;

(b) the market position of the undertakings concerned and their economic and financial power, the opportunities available to suppliers and users, their access to supplies or markets, any legal or other barriers to entry, supply and demand trends for the relevant goods and services, the interests of the intermediate and ultimate consumers, and the development of technical and economic progress provided that it is to consumers' advantage and does not form an obstacle to competition.

There is a certain inconsistency between these two paragraphs. Both place the emphasis on competition, but the second introduces a range of other, seemingly extraneous, factors. The genesis of the confusion lies in the history of the negotiation. Originally, paragraph (a) dealt with competition, and paragraph (b) with other matters of public interest. The latter was progressively watered down during the negotiations on the merger regulation as the emphasis behind the whole regulation switched more towards competition. Yet the legal uncertainty arises because mention is still made of these other criteria, which the regulation says 'the Commission shall take into account'. At one and the same time the regulation thus seeks to establish competition as the main criterion but also lists other factors which cannot be ignored. Its language is unsatisfactory from a legal point of view because it requires a large measure of further interpretation.

For example, it is at the very least debatable whether a merger control regulation should explicitly take up the interests of intermediate and ultimate consumers. In doing so, paragraph (b) implies that the Commission will have the right to introduce its own subjective interpretation of what consumer interests really are. They might, for example, be seen as having to do mainly with security of supply, which could be best assured by building up a Community-wide industry so that it could survive against foreign competition. Potentially, as a result of this wording, the Commission's decision-making could become less predictable and the basic competition criteria could end up being fudged.

Similarly, the admission of 'technical and economic progress' as an assessment criterion introduces a further element of uncertainty. The value of competition lies in the incentive it provides to firms to lower their costs and improve the quality of their output. The regulation does not make clear why and how the need to promote technical and economic progress is relevant to the merger control process. In practice it will be up to the Commission to determine when this becomes a relevant factor in assessing mergers. The weight it attaches to it will be crucial to the impact of the regulation.

The reference to technical and economic progress is drawn from Article 85(3) of the EEC Treaty. In past interpretations of this Article, the Commission has veered on the side of competition. It has used it as justification for granting derogations to the ban on restrictive business practices, but has limited these derogations to a specific period of time. It has no obligation to impose such a time-limit, however, and it is in any case impossible to permit a merger only for a limited period.

The working of this part of the regulation is thus open to a range of interpretations. Consequently, there is a strong risk that consistency and transparency will be lacking in its implementation, and that it will not always be clear how absolute the weight given to competition has been. The pro-competition thinking of the current Commission may not be matched by its successors. Contrary to what some in Brussels think, the number of cases dealt with during the present Commission's tenure is also unlikely to be large enough to build up a body of precedent that would tie the hands of future administrations.

The third, and last, fundamental point of controversy related to the question of whether the Commission should have the exclusive right to vet mergers. A primary objective of European industry was to reach an arrangement that provided 'one-stop shopping' and eliminated the risk that a favourable decision by one relevant authority would be countermanded by another. This raised awkward issues for the other parties involved, however. While the Commission could argue that a European approach was needed to secure a level playing-field and ensure consistency, several member states were reluctant to give up their national powers. It has been seen how this led to the establishment of high turnover thresholds for mergers deemed to have a Community-wide dimension. Among the other issues that also had to be decided was the question of exceptions. Were there cases where member states could override the Commission? Which cases should be included on such a list?

Here the position of Germany is once again important. Both Germany and the United Kingdom resisted the idea of giving the Commission exclusive competence for regulating mergers during the long discussions which led up to the new regulation. But their reasons were rather different. Even though it relies heavily on competition criteria when making national decisions on mergers, the United Kingdom wanted to retain the right to take what it regarded as matters of legitimate public interest into account. It did not want to grant the Community exclusive competence in this area. Germany had at one point been prepared to give the Commission exclusive rights to vet mergers provided that competition factors were the yardstick. As it became clear that the talks were leading to the inclusion of a public-interest yardstick, the German government began to seek the right to overrule the Commission in order to protect its strict competition principles.

The final regulation takes some account of this concern. It allows for member states to re-examine mergers which have been passed by the Commission, but only in circumstances in which the potential effect was confined to a limited geographic market, such as retailing, within a particular member state, and where a concentration threatens to create or strengthen a dominant position on a distinct market, be it a substantial part of the common market or not. In practice, the Commission expects cases where this happens to be rare, making this clause only a tiny exception to the 'one-stop-shop' concept.

Of potentially greater significance in allowing member states to claw back powers from the Commission are the grounds set out in Article 21(3) of the regulation which restore controlling authority to member governments. Legitimate sovereign interests in this respect include plurality of media ownership and fulfilment of prudential regulations in sectors such as financial services. Also covered, however, are mergers with a bearing on the notoriously vague concept of 'public security'. A lax interpretation of this part of the regulation could have the effect of undermining the 'one-stop shop' in a number of cases. Even if the interpretation is narrow and concerned clearly with defence, it is still likely to mean the effective exclusion from European control of a sector in which large-scale restructuring is likely to occur as firms adjust to political developments in Eastern Europe.

The normal supposition about this part of the regulation is that public security effectively means defence, an area which is specifically reserved for member-state competence under the Treaty of Rome. The main body of jurisprudence established by the European Court goes in this direction. None the less the concept is not properly defined and any guidelines established by the Commission might be open to challenge. In the United States, the meaning of the words 'national security' is rather broad. National security was, for example, the justification advanced by the Department of Commerce for opposing the Fujitsu/Fairchild merger in 1987. Much European opposition to the Exon-Florio clause in the 1988 Omnibus Trade Act stems from the fact that it allows mergers to be opposed on precisely this vague ground. The new EC regulation confers on member states the possibility to oppose, on grounds of public security, mergers that might otherwise be passed by the Commission just at a time of strong opposition to Japanese industrial expansion in the Community. It is not unlikely that, in some member states, attempts will be made to use the public-security argument to prevent such Japanese expansion. If this happened, Europe would find itself embarked on a course which it has already bitterly criticized in the United States.

This analysis has revealed several inadequacies in the new regulation, even though on paper it still represents a considerable advance. The Community has finally been able, after sixteen years of struggle, to agree a common merger policy. The regulation holds out the prospect of a 'one-stop shop' with an established procedure which will give a more secure footing to Commission activity in this area than the flawed powers it currently possesses under Articles 85 and 86. Just as the Commission will receive exclusive powers to vet larger mergers, it will not seek to use Articles 85 and 86 to vet mergers falling outside the agreed thresholds. For the first time, too, there will be a pre-notification requirement, so that the Commission will have a speedier means of knowing what is going on.

On the other hand, the thresholds have been pitched so as to exclude all but the largest mergers. No more that 50 cases a year are expected to reach Brussels, according to the Commission. In practice the number may be only about half this total. Unless member states make large-scale use of their right under the regulation to refer small mergers to Brussels, which, as has been noted, is unlikely, there can be no talk as yet of a standard European approach. The diversity of treatment between member states is likely to continue for some time to come. Moreover, the imprecise way in which parts of the regulation are worded have raised uncertainty about how it will be applied. In theory the Commission has a considerable amount of leeway, but, because of the exemptions written into the regulation, so do the member states.

In short, the new regulation can be regarded as no more than an interim solution to a problem that has plagued the Community for years.

Outlook

Agreement on the new regulation is unlikely to halt the proliferation of anti-trust legislation and amendments to existing legislation at national level within the Community. The wave of mergers that developed during the 1980s in the run-up to the single market had already prompted governments to look afresh at this issue. Thus Germany decided to tighten its merger control provisions by amending its Act against Restraints of Competition, and both Portugal and Spain introduced new merger legislation at the end of 1988 and in summer 1989 respectively. Since the new regulation falls far short of transferring full competence to the Commission, this process is almost certain to continue, adding to the uncertainty facing business.

Later, however, as consensus develops about the application of the new European regulation, pressure will emerge for harmonization of laws at national level. Even West Germany's Cartel Office may find itself under pressure to abandon its rigorous dependence on pure competition criteria in assessing mergers. The new regulation creates a clear two-tier structure. Mergers in Germany that fall outside the threshold for Community competence will still be judged purely on the basis of their effect on competition. Larger mergers will be vetted by the Commission according to different criteria which contain ambiguities in their wording. There might thus be regulatory discrimination against smaller mergers. To avoid this the Federal Cartel Office in Berlin has indicated that it would not ban a merger if it seemed that Brussels would permit it. Here, too, the regulation may indirectly help to promote a standardized approach across the Community.

Yet one of the largest worries surrounding the implementation of the new regulation remains the administrative burden it will place on the Commission itself. Even before it was agreed the Commission was heavily stretched. In its 'Eighteenth Report on Competition Policy' for 1988, published in October 1989, as well as in preceding reports, the Commission lists a high number of cases pending and admits to difficulties in clearing the backlog. At the end of 1988, a total of 3,451 cases were awaiting administrative treatment,* slightly more than the figure of 3,427 posted for the previous year. In its Sixteenth report (for 1986), the Commission said the backlog was 'regrettable, but inevitable, given the numbers of staff as compared with the volume of work'. Since the Competition Directorate settles an average of less than 400 cases per year, it would have to work for almost nine years to clear the backlog.

As a first step the Commission needs a substantial increase in manpower. One solution that has been suggested is that member states should second some of their own specialists to the Commission for a limited period so that the backlog can be cleared. There has been talk of between 40 and 50 officials being added to the team in this way, but this may still not be enough. Even with the additional help there is a risk that the Commission will face problems meeting the tough schedules mandated by the new regulation. These call for its investigation to be completed at the latest five months after notification. With such tight time-scales there is a danger that corners will be cut. Member states will not be able to follow developments closely in the Advisory Council, so they will frequently have to give the Commission the benefit of the doubt. The Commission's work will be all the harder insofar as it will deal only with cases involving large companies. Since these will normally be multi-product companies, it will need an examination of several different product markets as well as

---

*This figure covers all cases dealt with by the Directorate under Articles 85 and 86 of the EEC Treaty and Articles 65 and 66 of the ECSC Treaty, not just those dealing with mergers.

different regions within the Community before a decision on a proposed merger can be made.

However, it is not just a simple question of manpower. The hierarchy and decision-making process within the Commission also give cause for concern. Four different sections of DGIV, the Directorate General that deals with competition, may become involved before a case can be decided by the Director General concerned. Thereafter, decisions have to be made on a further three levels before a case has finally completed its journey through the administrative pipeline: it must be reviewed by the Commission's Legal Service, by the Advisory Committee of member states, and finally by the entire 17-person Commission, which must vote on the decision. This process is further complicated by the difficulty of translating the relevant documents into nine official languages. The whole process is structured in such a way that will make it difficult for balanced decisions to be reached within the stipulated time-scale. This cumbersome procedure holds the seeds of another controversy. With such a broad flow of information between so many parties, it will be almost impossible to prevent leaks and insider trading. Although insider trading remains legal in some member states, it is bound to cause problems with others, not to mention the United States if an American company should become involved.

Conclusion: a separate authority?
The idea of scheduling a review of the regulation after its first four years of operation was to allow time to test its effectiveness. Only after member states had seen how the Commission operated the regulation in practice, and how well it was able to mesh in with the operations of national authorities, were they prepared to transfer to it greater authority. For the time being the transfer of responsibility is grudging. This explains both the high turnover thresholds and the elaborate arrangements for member states to claw back their authority in cases that involve questions of public interest other than competition. Underlying the complex structure this has imposed on the regulation is the old debate about how to define appropriate criteria for assessing mergers. Only a little bit further below the surface is the more general problem about how far member states can be expected to transfer their sovereign

power to the Commission. These difficulties have not been resolved in the regulation: they have only been glossed over.

This chapter has identified several problems relating to the new regulation. First, the high thresholds above which Community control applies mean that it will be impossible to speak of a common European standard for assessing corporate concentrations. Only the largest mergers will be caught up in the Community process. The others, including most of those affecting small member states, will remain under the jurisdiction of national governments. Some, for example West Germany, will apply a stricter competition yardstick than that mandated to the Commission in the regulation. Others, such as France, may concentrate more on other public-interest questions. Initially, at least, there will thus be discrimination in the way that different mergers are treated by different authorities, although over time this could lead to pressure for closer harmonization. Meanwhile, the wording of the regulation is imprecise, and this may lead to different interpretations of the extent to which criteria not directly related to competition, such as 'technical and economic progress', can be taken into account. Similarly, national authorities may override the Commission for reasons of 'public security', a notoriously vague concept. Finally, there is an organizational problem. The Commission may simply not be equipped to carry out the duties assigned to it under the regulation.

These considerations mean that the review of the regulation scheduled for 1994 will probably have to encompass more radical revisions than a simple lowering of the thresholds. If the maintenance of a competitive environment is to be a key object in the long run, it may eventually be necessary to consider establishing an independent authority. This is a view that, for different reasons, has already found favour in some quarters in West Germany and the United Kingdom. The European Parliament, too, passed a resolution on competition policy in January 1990, requiring the Commission to present a proposal for the transfer of merger control powers to a new European Cartel Office. The proposal is to be ready for debate when the new regulation is reviewed in four years' time, even though the Parliament itself acknowledges that it will take many more years to complete such a change. It would require an amendment to the Treaty itself, and that requires the unanimous agreement of member states.

What might be considered is a two-tier approach. At the first stage, an independent Community competition authority would, as far as possible, assess all mergers presented to it by a purely competitive yardstick. It would prohibit any merger which was expected to result in a dominant market position. At the second stage, the enterprises involved would be entitled to challenge its decisions before the European Court of Justice, or to apply to the Commission for an exemption to be granted on certain public-policy criteria.

This dual process would have the great advantage of transparency. The more controversial the merger case, the more difficult it often becomes for outsiders to perceive whether the main issue is competition or another matter of public interest. What is needed in such cases is an unambiguous picture of the effect on competition. Then at least it would be clear what the cost has been if, after considering the balance of its priorities, the Commission were to decide to grant an exemption. Public awareness of that cost would make the Commission ponder long and hard before reaching any decision to allow an exemption. In the end it might do so only rarely, but at the very least it would be spared pressure from vested interests to reach a particular decision by fudging its interpretation of an ambiguously worded regulation.

There would, however, also be some drawbacks. First, the process would be time-consuming and that could be to the disadvantage of the parties concerned. Second, it would involve the creation of a new institution which, as things stand at present, would be bound to be highly controversial. Such an institution would wield considerably less power than a European Central Bank and its mandate would be strictly limited. None the less, it would, as the Parliament acknowledged, require an amendment to the EEC Treaty before it could be established. The chances are that this would require years of negotiation and compromise during which any hope of establishing a strict competition yardstick would evaporate.

Moreover, the idea of creating a special institution to vet mergers raises the question of whether it would also be responsible for other competition policy activities, such as controlling cartels and restrictive practices. With only partial responsibility for making determinations on competition policy matters, an independent body could appear rather flimsy. To seek to transfer a full range of responsibilities to it would, however, add to the political obstacles in the way of its creation. Control of restrictive practices under Articles 85 and 86 is seen by the Commission as a central part of its activity and it would not easily relinquish decision-making powers in this area. One alternative might be for the Commission to appoint an advisory panel to assess the competitive impact of mergers. This would not necessitate a change in the Treaty, because its mandate would be purely to make recommendations and it would still be up to the Commission to make the actual decisions. However, an advisory panel would be weaker and more easily overridden than a fully-fledged independent authority.

For the time being, therefore, Europe will have to live with the new regulation in the hope that it will come up to the expectations of its supporters, and set, by precedent, a clear pro-competition yardstick for assessing mergers. Much depends on the way the Commission operates the regulation in practice, but it would be rash to underestimate the pressure to which it will be subjected. The risks are considerable that the new regulation will bring little advance in practice and that eventually Europe will once again become embroiled in a new debate about merger policy.

For all its emphasis on competition, the new regulation has too many loopholes and is too lacking in transparency. Sixteen years of debate have failed to resolve one of the most important questions, that of whether competition or public interest should be the main yardstick. It may well be that the Community could never agree to a mechanism that totally excluded consideration of public interest. An independent authority would incorporate a safety valve in this regard. Enterprises could ask the Commission to override a decision by the new authority on the grounds of public interest. Such requests would, no doubt, be made from time to time, but where they were granted it would be clear to all and sundry that the final decision had deviated from the central principle of retaining competition as the yardstick for assessing mergers.

Critics of this approach point out that it is similar to that in force at a national level in Germany where the merger between MBB and Daimler-Benz was permitted on public-interest grounds. They say that such an administrative structure for merger control is cumbersome and, because of MBB/Daimler-Benz, achieves little in the end. Yet, as already noted, there have been very few cases in Germany where the Economics Ministry has set aside a Cartel Office ruling. The MBB/Daimler-Benz case has been subject to wide public debate, and the final decision was therefore made with the maximum transparency.

With a similar system in force at the European level, there would be no disguising the fact that the objective of free competition had been sacrificed each time the Commission agreed to go against the European Cartel Office and permit a merger for public policy reasons. The case for doing so would have to be exceptionally strong. Only by making it hard for public interest to be taken into account will the Community develop an approach to mergers capable of achieving the basic objective – that of ensuring that the gains from the single market are maximized through the free play of market forces.

Notes

1 Decision by the European Court of Justice in the case 6/72 Continental Can Company Inc., Europemballage Corporation, *Official Journal of the European Communities*, C68, 21 August 1973, p. 33.

2 *Memorandum on Concentration*, Competition Series, Study no. 3, Brussels, 1966.

3 For a more detailed analysis of this case, see *Seventeenth Report on Competition Policy*, Commission of the European Communities, Brussels, 1988, p. 93ff. Also *Merger Control in the EEC*, Kluwer Law and Taxation Publishers, Deventer, Netherlands, 1988, p. 263ff.

4 See Stephen Woolcock, *European Mergers: National or Community Controls?*, RIIA Discussion Paper 15, Royal Institute of International Affairs, London, 1989.

3

CURBING SUBSIDIES

Joseph Gilchrist and David Deacon*

The maintenance of a system of free and undistorted competition is one of the cornerstones of the European Economic Community. The founders of the original common market recognized right from the outset that financial help given to companies by member governments could be used to frustrate competition. The risk was that subsidies – or state aids, as they are commonly called – would replace tariffs and the other forms of protection that were to be progressively abolished inside the new Europe. The Treaty of Rome therefore established a powerful system of control, going beyond the disciplines agreed under the General Agreement on Tariffs and Trade (GATT), whereby national state aids would be monitored by the Commission.

But, at the same time, the Treaty makes allowance for national state aids to have a positive effect on the development of the Community. If properly controlled, they might, for example, help develop backward regions or finance extra research-and-development efforts. In this way, Community goals for which the Commission itself lacked the necessary financial resources could be promoted.

* The authors work in the Directorate for State Aids, Directorate General for Competition of the Commission of the European Communities. The views expressed are those of the authors and not necessarily those of the Commission.

31

Curbing subsidies

This chapter looks at how the Commission will and should respond, in the light of this dichotomy, to the extra challenge created by the single market. The level of state aids is already very high in the Community. Faced with the burden of restructuring to meet additional competition in the single market, more firms are likely to seek assistance from their governments. Although the Commission has considerable powers to control state aids, it lacks manpower and has failed in the past to deal forcefully with those aids which distort trade and competition the most. It will be argued here that policy needs to be refocused towards the larger companies which receive most in the form of aids. Even so, it will be difficult to get to grips with some of the more fashionable forms of aids, such as those directed towards research and development.

The idea that state aids can have both a negative and a positive impact is clear from Articles 92 and 93 of the Treaty of Rome, which lay down the principles under which the Commission controls state aids (see Appendix I). Article 92 bans 'any aid granted by a Member State or through State resources in any form whatsoever which distorts or threatens to distort competition by favouring certain undertakings or the production of certain goods'. However, this basic ban is followed by a list of aids which are admissible: those of a social character, those to make good damage caused by natural disasters, and those approved by the West German government to offset the economic disadvantages caused by the division of Germany after World War II.

Still more important exceptions to the general ban on aids are made in Article 92(3). This states that the Commission may consider the following categories of aid to be compatible with the aims of the common market: aid which promotes the economic development of areas suffering from abnormally low standards of living or serious underemployment; aid which promotes important projects of common European interests, or remedies a serious disturbance in the economy of a member state; and, finally, that which facilitates economic development in ways which do not conflict with the common European interest. It is the Commission, not the member states, that decides where one of these derogations can be granted.

Article 93 also lays down three procedures which form the basis of the Commission's power to control national state aids:

- Member states must give prior notification to the Commission of any plan to grant or alter the grant of aid. Only if the Commission approves the notified aid can it be put into operation.
- The Commission shall, in cooperation with each member state, keep under constant review all existing aid schemes. If warranted by the development needs of the common market, the Commission shall address appropriate measures to the member state concerned.
- These two procedures are linked by the so-called 'examination and contradictory procedure' which, after due process, allows the Commission, subject to appeal to the European Court of Justice, to modify or suppress a national aid.

In carrying out its control functions, the Commission does not in practice scrutinize every single aid award by each member state. Instead, it approves the general framework and conditions of aid schemes. Member states are then free to make awards within the limits of the approved scheme. Only in exceptional cases, such as those involving very sensitive sectors or large individual rescue operations, does the Commission examine awards to individual recipients.

In the years immediately following the oil-shock of the 1970s, aids were viewed more favourably in some quarters and were seen as a tool that could be used to promote economic adjustment.[1] Nowadays, the emphasis is more usually placed on their negative effects, particularly in the context of the internal market. This reflects a fundamental change in attitude towards state aids by certain member states, notably the United Kingdom and the Netherlands, where it is government policy to reduce the role of the state in the economy.

An economic case for using state aids as a policy instrument can be made only if the cost of intervening to correct a market failure is outweighed by the benefits of such intervention to society as a whole. It is very difficult, however, for governments to identify such occasions. Moreover, studies in the United States have shown that it costs substantially more than $1 in lost output to raise $1 in tax revenue, because taxation acts as a disincentive to economic activity and its impact is therefore never neutral. The same must be true of the EC, where marginal tax rates are higher. When the administrative costs of granting aid, together with the resources companies expend to obtain it, are taken into account, the benefits to society would have to be substantial for aid to be economically worthwhile.[2]

Left to themselves, there is always the risk that member states will use aids to try to export some of their own problems. Governments take account only of their own national interests in granting aids and this can rapidly lead to problems. For example, unfair subsidies in one country can lead to unemployment in another, prompting calls for countervailing aids.

At the national level, state aids can be used in a number of different ways. They may be applied defensively to rescue companies in difficulty, or they can be used to support aggressive trade policies, for example in the field of research and development or for direct help to investment. Yet, however they are applied, they risk leading to the same result: the creation of national champion industries which are able to pre-empt an unfair share of economic resources, regardless of the cost to the Community as a whole. There is thus a real danger that the combined effect of independently applied national policies could lead to incoherent, contradictory and unfair results at Community level.

Only firm Community control can ensure that any benefits obtained from state aids outweigh the resulting distortion of competition in the common market. The need for strict control is why this is one of the few areas in which the Commission, rather than the Council of Ministers, has the real and effective power, subject only to appeal to the European Court of Justice.

The influence of 1992
The completion of the single market by the end of 1992, and the projected development of Economic and Monetary Union (EMU) thereafter, reinforce the need for an effective competition policy, particularly in the field of state aids. Such aids are a threat to the very unity of the common market, since they can be used to replace barriers to trade that have been dismantled in the integration process or to give other artificial advantages. Without proper control, state aids could impede the optimum allocation of

resources, which is both the main benefit of the single market and the main purpose behind its creation.

The indiscriminate use of state aids by member states could also undermine efforts that are being made to promote regional development, and thus greater economic and social cohesion across the Community, by means of loans from the Community's structural funds. Given the volume of resources available in the richer member states, state aids in these countries could easily offset the benefits derived by the poorer peripheral states from the structural funds. In the period 1981-6, state aids to industry were roughly ten times the size of the structural funds. Even after the projected doubling of the structural funds to around Ecu 15bn in connection with the 1992 programme, they will still amount, at most, to just one-fifth of present state aids to industry.

The completion of the internal market implies a further intensification of competition, which will in turn necessitate structural change in the economies of member states. Only then can the full benefits of the market integration process be obtained. Even if the volume of state aids stays the same, their impact on trade and competition will become greater because other trade barriers are being brought down and competition is intensifying. Moreover, there is a danger that member states could use state aids to protect certain industries from the full force of competition. As a result, current industrial structures would fossilize; not every industry in every country can be a winner, and those that appear to be falling behind are likely to appeal to their governments for help. This danger is all the greater, since state aids will soon be the only remaining instrument of protection available to member states against intra-Community competition. The other forms of protection, such as preferential public procurement for national suppliers or product standards designed to disadvantage imports, are being dismantled in the run-up to 1992. Without a firm and comprehensive aid policy there can therefore be no real internal market. Such a policy is in the interest of member states. The poorer ones do not have the resources to compete with richer members. For the latter to compete in granting aid would amount to a beggar-my-neighbour policy. This is a negative-sum game, and costly in terms of budget and inflation.

The state aids survey
In view of the importance of aids to the completion of the internal market, the Commission decided to conduct a review of policy. As a first step, it initiated a major exercise to identify the volume, trend and form of all state aids in all member states.[3]

To start with volume, the survey showed that in 1988 the total annual volume of state aids in all member states amounted to around £60bn (Ecu 85bn), which represents 2.5 per cent of gross domestic product, or £490 per employed person. State aids exceed direct taxes on companies and constitute an important factor in the budget deficit of certain member states, notably Italy and Belgium. The amounts are so high that their impact, not just on competition but more broadly on the economy as a whole, cannot be ignored.

In most member states, around half the aid is given to agriculture, fisheries, coal and railways. These sectors receive massive subsidies. On average in 1986-8, railways received £19bn, or 29 per cent of value added; coal £9bn, or £15,000 per employee; and agriculture £7bn, or 11 per cent of value added. This last figure represents purely national aid. Agriculture received a further £18bn from direct Community intervention.

Special policy considerations apply to these sectors, however. Farm subsidies are inextricably bound up with the whole working of the Common Agricultural Policy. Transport subsidies are permitted under Article 77 of the EEC Treaty. Coal comes under the European Coal and Steel Community, and does not in any case figure large in intra-Community trade: Belgium has closed its last mine, France is running down its production, and only West Germany, the United Kingdom and Spain are significant producers. There are important social and energy policy issues at stake in Germany, where the so-called Jahrhundertvertrag (Hundred-Year Agreement) guarantees the purchase of German coal by the electricity supply industry. This particular issue is dealt with in the following chapter, which is concerned with the regulation of monopoly utilities; here we shall restrict ourselves to examining the impact on the single market of aids to the manufacturing and service sectors.

Manufacturing in fact receives almost all the state aids not swallowed by farming, fisheries, coal and railways. On average in 1986-8, state aids to manufacturing amounted to nearly 4 per cent of value added, or £1,016 per employee. Within manufacturing two sectors stood out: in 1981-5 steel accounted for £4bn in subsidies, or 36 per cent of value added, while shipbuilding took £900m, or 26 per cent of value added. These sectors are, however, now handled within special Community-aid frameworks, which lay down clear and strict rules for the granting of aid.[4] In the case of steel there has been an enormous reduction in aid volumes now that necessary restructuring has been completed. Even Italy's Bagnoli plant is scheduled for closure by the end of 1990. Only limited aids are now allowed for plant closures, research and development, and investments in environmental protection. Shipbuilding is governed by an aid code negotiated in the multilateral framework of the Organization for Economic Cooperation and Development (OECD), although large volumes of aid are still granted that in general are directly related to the volume of ships constructed. In December 1989, the Commission unveiled a plan to cut maximum aid to shipbuilders from 26 per cent to 20 per cent of production costs. It said it would be prepared to phase out subsidies to shipbuilders altogether, although this was conditional on the adoption of a fairer pricing policy by Japan and South Korea.

A further point revealed by the survey was the wide difference in aid volume granted by individual member states. This is illustrated in Table 3.1, which shows that, excluding aid to steel and shipbuilding, Italy, with 6.5 per cent, gave around twice as much in relation to value added between 1986 and 1988 as France, the United Kingdom and Germany. Of the smaller states, both Greece and Ireland gave a significant volume of aid as a per-centage of value added. In both these countries aid has, however, been reduced substantially by the abolition under Community pressure of important tax concessions for exports. Of the remaining states, Denmark stands out as well below average, with only 1.6 per cent of value added.

To move on to the trends in aid, once again excluding steel and shipbuilding, the survey showed that here, too, there had been great variation among member states. In 1981 France, the United Kingdom and Germany gave approximately the same amount of aid in cash terms at roughly £3.2bn apiece (1981 prices); Italy's budget was nearly 50 per cent higher at £5bn. Over the period 1981-8, France's budget started to decline after an initial rise, that

37

of the United Kingdom declined sharply, Germany's crept slowly upwards and Italy's declined slightly in real terms. Thus, in 1988, the United Kingdom gave £2.3bn (in 1987 prices), France £3.3bn, Germany £5.5bn and Italy £6.6bn – nearly three times as much as the United Kingdom.* These results on their own show how urgent is the need for a policy review.

Table 3.1 Aids to manufacturing: average 1986-8 (average 1981-6), 1987 prices

Country	As % of value added*	£ per worker*	Ecu per worker*	As % of value added in steel 1981-5	As % of value added in shipbuilding 1981-6
Italy	6.7 (8.2)	2,174 (2,678)	3,077 (3,791)	71.4	34.2
Greece	16.4 (13.9)	2,629 (n.a.)	3,721 (n.a.)	n.a.	n.a.
Ireland	6.2 (7.1)	1,802 (1,802)	2,551 (2,551)	107.2	n.a.
Belgium	4.6 (4.5)	1,196 (1,083)	1,693 (1,533)	40.4	27.7
Netherlands	3.5 (4.1)	969 (988)	1,371 (1,399)	4.3	10.7
France	3.5 (3.6)	1,080 (1,019)	1,528 (1,442)	58.3	56.6
Luxembourg	4.4 (3.5)	1,280 (791)	1,812 (1,119)	14.6	—
UK	2.5 (2.9)	510 (614)	723 (868)	57.6	21.6
W. Germany	2.7 (2.9)	804 (714)	1,134 (1,010)	8.6	12.3
Denmark	1.6 (2.8)	454 (495)	643 (700)	18.0	33.8
Spain	3.7 (—)	754 (—)	1,067 (—)	—	—
Portugal	8.1 (—)	495 (—)	701 (—)	—	—
EC 12	3.8 (4.0)	1,016 (1,080)	1,439 (1,474)	36.0	26.0

Source: Commission of the European Communities, *Survey of State Aids.*
* Excluding steel and shipbuilding.

Despite the effort that went into the survey, the Commission still lacks information in a number of areas. There are, for example, no comprehensive figures on the regional and sectoral impact of state aids. Consequently, apart from certain sensitive areas in which special sectoral frameworks have been or are in operation (e.g. steel, shipbuilding, synthetic fibres, textiles and cars), the Commission cannot determine whether Community goals are

*The figure for France was artificially inflated by one large ad hoc payment to a single company. The actual underlying figure was £2.3bn. Over half Germany's aid was to West Berlin alone.

being negated by the impact of national state aids. Thus it cannot tell whether aid spent on the legitimate Community goal of regional development is being offset by a concentration of subsidies for research and development in prosperous and overcrowded areas. Neither does it at present have adequate information on the total aid going to individual large companies from the cumulative impact of the many different schemes in operation.

The survey did show, however, that most aid for manufacturing does not come from funds with a specially designated regional or sectoral development purpose. Instead it is concentrated in what are called 'horizontal aids', such as those for research-and-development, aids to small and medium enterprises, and aids for exports to third countries. Horizontal aids, which are generally less transparent than other forms of aid, have grown in importance, since member states have been using them to intervene in an increasing number of areas.

Finally, the survey revealed two other significant facts. First, aids to declining sectors and for the rescue of ailing industries have taken more of the aid budget than aids for industries of the future, despite the relative importance of aids for research and development.* Second, there are over 1,000 known aid schemes in operation in the Community. This figure excludes schemes operated by any of the estimated 36,000 local authorities.

Immediate policy implications
In addition to the very high overall levels of aid and its particular concentration in certain member states, the survey pointed towards another conclusion with immediate policy implications. A number of areas stood out where member states spend large sums but where to date the control exercised by the Commission has been limited or not very effective. They include: general investment aids, export credit and insurance, aids to rescue companies in difficulties, and capital injections and other flows into public-sector companies. In dealing with these areas, the

---

*A word of caution is necessary about figures for R&D aid, since only direct subsidies are counted. Any aid element in R&D 'contracts', defence expenditure, or the funding of public and semi-public research institutes are excluded, even though the funds involved dwarf direct subsidies. The Commission plans to make these excluded elements the subject of further study.

Commission has already adopted the approach of developing greater transparency before applying controls. This classic approach has already produced the framework on state aids for research and development, which came into effect in 1986 and is scheduled for review in 1991.

General investment schemes
These are schemes with no specific sectoral or regional objectives. Their volume has grown rapidly. On the face of it they have become a discretionary investment stimulus incompatible with the needs of the internal market. Such aid constitutes one of the tools of the nationalist industrial policy which, as has been shown above, can conflict with agreed Community goals as well as distort trade and competition.

Work has begun on analysing the major schemes. Either they have already been reviewed by the Commission, in which case measures are being addressed to the member states concerned under Article 93(1), or they have not been notified. In the latter case they can be treated as non-notified aids, information can be demanded and, where appropriate, the procedure of Article 93(2), which allows the Commission to modify or suppress a national aid, can be brought into force.

Export credits
The Commission has always adopted a strict policy in respect of aids to export credits in intra-Community trade. Medium-term official credits or guarantees on such business are banned. Special considerations apply to credits for exports outside the Community; they are covered by the multilateral 'Consensus' arrangement in the OECD, to which the European Community subscribes. Article 112 of the Treaty of Rome also provides for the progressive harmonization of the terms under which member states grant aid for exports to third countries. This article does not, however, appear to prevent the application of Article 92 when it can be shown that aids to exports outside the Community have an impact, albeit indirectly, on trade and competition inside the common market. Until now, other priorities have prevented this secondary effect on internal trade being examined in detail from the angle of competition policy. Given the sums involved and the wide

differences between member states, export credits now need scrutiny. The Commission has made a start by requiring member states to notify their existing schemes. In particular, they have to provide information on which of their exporters were the chief beneficiaries. The links between export credits and overseas aid will also have to be examined in the context of the continuing discussion in the OECD.

Rescue of major ailing companies

In practically all cases of rescue of major ailing companies, whatever the industrial sector, the Commission has approved all, or the major part, of the aid. Even though such a decision may have appeared justified in the light of short-term economic, social and political factors, the effect may often have been to retard real restructuring in the industry concerned. International competitiveness will have suffered as a result.

There is also here a possible conflict with regional policy objectives. Aid used to rescue companies in the richer, central regions of the Community can strengthen those regions at the expense of the poorer peripheral regions. Industry is thus deprived of an incentive to relocate. By contrast, there may be a case for preserving for a limited time ailing economic structures in the regions, where resources cannot easily be redeployed and a longer period is needed for adjustment.

Aid disciplines in rescue cases must be tightened up and account must be taken of the regional dimension. Otherwise rescue schemes risk becoming an obstacle to the industrial restructuring which is an essential part of the market integration process unleashed by the 1992 programme.

Capital injection into public-sector companies

Commission policy in this area was published in *Bulletin of the European Communities*, No. 9, 1984. It rests on the broad principle that a capital injection financed with state resources counts as a state aid if it would not be undertaken by a private investor under the same circumstances and conditions. Such injections are subject to Articles 92 and 93 of the Treaty of Rome. This policy declaration is backed by two transparency directives, which can be used to make available the information required.[5]

Some big individual cases have been examined, but many of them have come to light only after the fact as a result of information contained in the press,* rather than through prior notification by member states in accordance with their obligation under Article 93. Effective intervention to prevent distortion of trade and competition has thus been difficult. The survey of state aids also revealed a considerable volume of capital injections that appear to constitute aid and have never been notified or treated as such. Admittedly, large private-sector companies may decide for sound policy reasons to support loss-making operations over relatively long periods. Public-sector companies are entitled to behave in the same way, but such interventions may be disguised rescue operations of ailing companies or could be used to promote a national industrial policy. Aid discipline in this area will have to be reinforced to monitor more effectively all types of financial transactions between the state and public enterprises, in particular to ensure that prior notification is given.

The need for longer-term change
Despite the short-run policy changes that are now either under study or under way as a result of the survey, there is also a growing feeling that more far-reaching change is needed. The new situation created by the completion of the internal market calls for a policy that has clearer direction, coherence and transparency. This notion has been reinforced by the size of the aid programmes revealed by the survey and by the differences between member states. Questions that need to be addressed in this context concern not only the economic costs of state aids, but also the way in which control is exercised by the Commission.

In the past, state aid policy has focused on the primary objectives of aid schemes (e.g. regional aids, aids for energy saving, aids to small and medium-sized enterprises). The work of the Commission is organized in such a way that its main aim is to determine whether the objective of a particular scheme qualifies it for a derogation from the general ban on aids. The practice of member states also conforms to this approach. As a result, too little attention has been paid to the analysis of the underlying

---

*A case in point would be the purchase in 1988 of Alfa Romeo by Fiat, which was found to have involved aid.

impact of state aids on competition, of regional and sectoral cross-effects, and of the cumulative benefits for large recipients. A shift of emphasis is needed if more effective control is to be exercised. Aid schemes should be judged less on whether they qualify technically for a derogation and more on their effect on trade and competition, even when they involve a rescue operation for a politically sensitive large company.

Such a shift could lead to an increase in the number of schemes blocked by the Commission in the run-up to 1992. Currently only 2 to 3 per cent are turned down. In tightening up, however, the Commission could argue that it is simply following a fundamental principle of Community policy. Article 3(f) of the Treaty of Rome provides for the institution of a system of undistorted competition. Both the general terms of the EEC Treaty and the structure of Article 92 recognize that other policy objectives are secondary to the competition objective.

The Commission's practice of emphasizing the primary object of aid – without highlighting either its sectoral or its regional impact on the recipient of the vast bulk of the aid – makes it possible that certain Community objectives are being countervailed. For example, development policy directed towards the poorer peripheral regions may be contradicted by the regional effect of research-and-development aids that are concentrated in the central regions. The fact that, once the Commission approves most aid schemes, national authorities will have discretionary powers in granting aid to whomsoever they wish, increases the possibility that aid policy may be used to subvert stated Community priorities.

It is easier to see the distortions of competition and trade in cases where the recipient of aid is identified. This happens only in larger cases and they are exceptional, relating mostly to the rescue of companies in trouble. Even here, the Commission has shied away from considering the effect on competition when making its decision. Hardly ever has it blocked aid to a large company. In most cases it has been willing to agree aid, albeit in smaller amounts than those originally proposed and on the condition that some limited restructuring takes place. However, it has neither the staff nor the legal means to verify whether an agreed restructuring plan is actually implemented. Its powers in this area are considerably less than those under the anti-trust Articles 85 and

86, which have implementing regulations and powers of inspection.

Some in the Commission argue that aid to companies which keeps them afloat enhances competition because these companies remain players in the market. However, it would be wrong to assume that the choice in all cases is between aid with restructuring or total closure. The assets of the ailing concern will be put on the market and some jobs may be saved. In the United Kingdom, for example, Rolls-Royce was allowed to go under but its fortunes are now restored. Rover enjoyed billions of pounds worth of subsidies prior to privatisation, but employment there still declined. It is conceivable that as many jobs have been lost with aid as would have gone without it.

The largest rescue schemes have often involved public-sector companies where the Commission has come under political pressure to approve state aids. Its failure to block such rescue schemes has allowed member states artificially to preserve their ailing national champions. The price is often a fragmentation of European industry along national lines and a consequent loss of international competitiveness, which may lead to renewed pressure for state aids in the future. Too many sectors in the Community are still largely organized along national lines. A further point about public-sector companies is the difficulty experienced by the Commission in monitoring their financial relationship with the state. Its application of state aids policy towards them has not been fully effective because it has found it hard to detect hidden state aids.

Finally, the Commission is understaffed; it has fewer than three dozen senior officials dealing with state aids across the whole of the Community. In the Walloon region of Belgium alone, there are 150 people involved in granting aids. The result of this unequal balance is that the Commission has to concentrate its resources. It has given priority to the steady flow of new notifications of aid schemes mandated by the Treaty. These newly notified aids do not, however, constitute the majority of aid being granted. Tying up scarce administrative resources in this way reduces the scope for monitoring old schemes that were approved long ago or for tracking down those that were never approved at all. This is where the bulk of aid is concentrated. For an administration as overstretched as the Commission, it is difficult to search actively for harmful schemes and take controversial decisions to block them. The easy way out is to home in on the notification of new schemes by member states, but this will become even less satisfactory in view of the heightened importance of competition policy after 1992.

At the same time, however, the Commission has to be wary of becoming over-bureaucratic. It cannot possibly expect to pass judgment on the countless small aid schemes in operation around the Community. Literally thousands of such schemes, generally administered by local authorities, are coming to light as a result of the restructuring of regional funds that are now used to co-finance them. These schemes have little or no effect on intra-Community trade. To oppose them on grounds of competition policy would contravene the spirit of the EEC Treaty as well as the generally accepted principle of subsidiarity whereby the Commission concerns itself only with matters that actually need to be dealt with at a European level. One solution would be to absolve member states from the requirement to notify the Commission of all the smaller aids, which have no real or appreciable impact on intra-Community trade and competition. For example, notification might be scrapped for aids which involve less than Ecu 50,000 per beneficiary firm.

This would free administrative resources to examine more critically the existing aid schemes and those large cases that actually do threaten to distort trade and competition or prevent restructuring of industry. The incidence of negative decisions is meanwhile likely to increase. Since many will be formally challenged by the member state concerned, the Commission will have to prepare its case more carefully than at present. This is an additional reason why it should concentrate on essentials for, and after, 1992.

Ways to adapt policy for 1992

There are thus three main areas in which the Commission should redirect its efforts: ensuring that large aid schemes do not distort trade and competition, preventing aid schemes being used to promote national industrial policies, and ensuring that aids granted in the central regions do not conflict with regional policy.

The Commission must shift its emphasis away from concentrating on new notifications, to monitoring all aids with a significant impact. The appropriate legal instrument exists in Article 93(1), which obliges the Commission to keep the application of existing aid schemes under constant review. For this monitoring to be effective, the Commission must be in a position to know where aids are actually given, and able to evaluate their impact on trade and competition. This will necessitate further increases in the thresholds below which aid does not have to be notified, and a more detailed system of reporting by member states of large schemes. This will help determine the real sectoral and regional impact of aid to see that Community objectives are not being overturned. In particular, the Commission must ensure that aid is not being concentrated on a few recipients or in a few sectors where the impact on the conditions of competition is great. Closer scrutiny should be directed particularly at member states that give a disproportionately large or unwarranted volume of aid. It is in these reviews of existing schemes under Article 93(1) that the Commission could apply a policy of putting more emphasis on distortions of competition and trade coming from aid, and less on the policy objectives promoted.

The Commission must prevent aids being used to promote national industrial policies that lead to the preservation of local champions in each 'key' sector. Such aid has tended to fragment European industry, since it has been an obstacle in the way of market forces pushing for rationalization, with strong companies absorbing or overhauling weaker ones. Since publicly controlled enterprises and the rescue of ailing companies are often the instruments of national industrial policy, it is essential that the policy proposals advocating a stricter attitude in these fields become really effective.

The Commission will also have to pay careful attention to regional policy; indeed it cannot avoid doing so. Regional policy is specifically cited in Article 93 as a ground under which derogations to the general ban on aids can be permitted. It is also important to the success of the 1992 programme. The policy challenge for the Commission is thus to ensure that the regions are allowed to grant aids which make them attractive to new investment, without creating the over-capacity in individual sectors that would simply lead to new trade and competition problems. If the regions felt cut off from the benefits of the integration process, the relatively new political cement holding the Community together could be severely tested.

A useful approach would be to increase the relative impact of aid to the regions by clamping down on aid granted in the richer, central parts of the Community. Mobile new investment will not necessarily be attracted to the regions merely by increasing their already generous ceilings on investment aids. Their governments do not necessarily have the resources to spend anything like the maximum permitted by the Commission. Policy towards aids in the central regions should simply become tougher, rather than concentrating on aids with a specific regional impact, which constitute only 5 per cent of total aids. The regional impact of the other 95 per cent is unknown, but they are heavily concentrated in the central regions, and the structural funds are far too small to afford real compensation. In a fully federal system, compensatory budgetary resources would flow automatically from rich to poor regions, but this is not even on the distant horizon for the Community.

A radical administrative approach may meanwhile be needed to ensure that aid is not concentrated in larger companies operating in the central regions of the Community. One such approach might be to concentrate on the 1,500 biggest firms in the Community, which account for over two-thirds of value added in manufacturing and an even greater proportion of intra-Community trade. Since aid to such companies is likely to have a disproportionate impact on trade and competition, they should be subject to more detailed control, with more general rules applying to the remaining companies. The benefits they receive will be at least partially highlighted in the system of reports now being instituted. Further work will be required, however, on the development of new monitoring methods, as well as on policy instruments and a suitable legal basis for control.

Limiting detailed control of state aids to large companies would mean that the Commission was, in effect, applying to the state-aid field the concept of 'appreciable effect' on trade and competition that it already applies to anti-trust policy. It would also simplify enforcement of the prior-notification requirement, thereby reducing the chances of aid being granted illegally and the attendant problem of recovery. The Commission has made increasing use of its powers to demand and enforce repayment of illegal aid, usually by converting it into a loan bearing commercial rates of interest. Yet it cannot undo the economic, trade and competition effect of the aid being granted in the first place. The most important benefit of aid – access to finance, and the resulting opportunity to survive or expand – cannot be undone.

How far, however, should the Commission go in seeking to control aid to large companies? At the tough end of the spectrum is the possibility of a total ban, although this would have to exclude regional aids and aids for R&D, since these are both permitted under Article 93. With such a ban in place, aids to other firms, such as small and medium enterprises (SMEs), might be allowed at the discretion of member governments up to limits strictly defined by the Commission. One possible drawback to this approach – the risk that large companies might still be able to obtain aid by applying for it in the name of a small subsidiary – is less of a problem than it appears. It could be dealt with by a provision in the rules that not more than 30 per cent of an SME may be held by another company.

None the less, there are other reasons why such an approach would be difficult to implement at present. It would be too rigid and indiscriminate in its application. It is also far from clear whether the Commission has the power to introduce such a strict policy without recourse to the Council of Ministers. Given the prevalence of state aids across the Community, it is unlikely that they would agree.

This suggests that there are limits to the Commission's ability to control state aids. Regional aids have been discussed at length above, but another sensitive area needs to be mentioned here: R&D aids. Into this area come the subsidies granted by member states for development of the European Airbus aircraft. These subsidies are, however, particularly controversial because of their impact on trade policy relationships with the United States, and they are dealt with as part of the discussion on trade policy in Chapter 5. The immediate aim here is to deal with the more general issue of R&D aids.

R&D aids are often regarded as the sacred cow of Community policy. It is doubly difficult to clamp down on them at national level because R&D programmes already operate at Community level. The idea of public finance for R&D enjoys strong support in the Community from those who believe it is needed to help Europe catch up with a perceived Japanese and US advantage in high technology. Its economic benefit is, however, unproven, and the volume of spending on R&D (including funds channelled through government contracts, over which the Commission currently has no control) is so high that it cannot be ignored. Not only is there a risk, as stated earlier, of R&D spending in the richer central states offsetting aid for regional development, but most R&D aid is probably spent on projects that would have gone ahead anyway. A key criterion in the framework on R&D aids was precisely this point of additionality. Yet it is virtually impossible for any member state, let alone the Commission, to check whether R&D aids have brought additional benefits. Even after the framework came into operation, Siemens and Philips were permitted to receive subsidies to develop their megachip. Both companies were cash-rich at the time; the technology was not new; and they would have had to develop the product anyway, with or without government funding.

In addition, R&D resources are expected to be in relatively inelastic supply in the short and medium term. There is a risk that aided projects will crowd out unaided ones without any real assurance of benefit. The main effect of aid is simply to strengthen the treasury of the company, rather than to stimulate extra R&D activity. Finally, R&D spending tends to be concentrated on a few large recipients in each member state and thus easily serves to promote national industrial policies.

These are all good reasons for tightening the net around R&D aids. Given the intense political difficulty of dealing with this type of aid, another approach could be examined. This would be the possibility of promoting R&D through tax concessions rather than through direct spending. A general reduction in corporate profits tax would leave companies with more resources at their disposal. They would be led by market forces in choosing whether or not to spend them on R&D and, if so, what projects to choose. Special tax treatment of R&D spending is less attractive, since it involves a conscious application of fiscal policy as a substitute for spending that has already been shown to be of doubtful value because of its distorting effect on trade and competition. Even this approach has the merit over direct spending in that it leaves companies more free to choose where to spend on R&D and minimizes bureaucratic interference.

Conclusion

In sum, it is clear that the existing system of controlling the distortion of trade and competition caused by state aids requires careful review if aids policy is to retain its credibility and adapt to the needs of 1992. There must be a shift of emphasis away from attempting to control all cases regardless of size and relying on new notifications of aids, towards a more selective role of examining the real impact of aids. Greater attention should be paid in this process to the aid received by large recipients, for it is here that governments are most likely to thwart the aims of the single market by pursuing national industrial policies that impede industrial rationalization and restructuring.

As part of its revised policy, the Commission will also have to increase the transparency of its role. At the moment it seeks out the opinion of other member states and interested third parties only in the limited number of cases in which doubts over the legality of the aid proposal prompt it to open the examination procedures in Article 93(2). Only limited information is made available to the public on aids which are approved. Yet it is precisely these decisions that actually distort competition. Not only is there virtually no legal mechanism for a firm to object to a decision by the Commission to approve the disbursal of aid to one of its competitors; firms may find it very difficult to establish what aid is actually being paid.

This contrasts markedly with the policy towards restrictive agreements and abuses under Articles 85 and 86 of the EEC Treaty, where the opinion of third parties is sought on all individual cases of anti-competitive agreements that the Commission intends to approve, as well as on general block exemptions.

To date there has been virtually no public debate in political, academic or business circles of policy towards state aids at the European level. One aim of this chapter has been to open up such debate. We have seen that, even with a stricter approach to aids, there are limits beyond which the Commission cannot go in its control effort, especially in the area of regional development and R&D. Yet some discipline must be applied to these areas, too, if the competitive environment of the single market is to be maintained. Greater transparency in handling aids policy should help ensure that this is indeed what happens.

Notes

1 See the Maldague Report, *Industrial Policies in the Community: State Intervention and Structural Adjustment*, Commission of the European Communities, Brussels, 1981. For further policy descriptions, see also the Commission's annual publication, *Report on Competition Policy*, (cf. ch. 2, n. 3, above). The chief legal instruments and policy documents relating to state aids have been published by the Commission in a volume entitled *Competition Rules in the EEC and ECSC Applicable to State Aids*, Brussels, 1987.

2 See C. L. Ballard, J. B. Shoren and J. Whalley, 'General Equilibrium Computation of the Marginal Welfare Cost of Taxes in the US', *The American Economic Review*, vol. 75 (1985), no. 1, pp. 128-38.

3 *First Survey on State Aids in the European Communities,* Commission of the European Communities, Brussels, 1989. The figures quoted come from an updated version, including Spain and Portugal, which was prepared in 1990.

4 For details, see conditions in the Sixth Directive on aids to shipbuilding, and the Regulation on state aids to the steel industry, in Appendix II.

5 *Official Journal of the European Communities*, no. L 195, 22 July 1980, and no. L 229, 28 August 1985.

4

REGULATING
THE UTILITIES

Peter Montagnon

One of the most important, and difficult, tasks for competition policy and the single market is that of coming to grips with utility services such as electricity, gas and water. In most Community countries these are state-sector monopolies. On the surface, the very idea of opening them up to competition is absurd, since their common feature is that they are all, to a greater or lesser degree, natural monopolies. Consumers do not enjoy a choice of water supply. When they turn on the tap in their houses, they take whatever water is in the pipe and pay the price that is charged. Short of massive expenditure in a duplicate distribution system, it could hardly be otherwise. The fear that the new owners of Britain's water industry could use this natural advantage to avoid giving value for money was behind much of the vehement opposition to water privatization in the United Kingdom. Behind the Commission's growing involvement in this area lies the realization that it has somehow to find a way of loosening the monopoly stranglehold held by the utilities. Otherwise the promised gains of the single market may not be realized.

This chapter examines the impact that the single market will have on the utilities. It is an area of particular challenge. Experience has already shown that almost any action taken or proposed by the Commission will risk bringing it into headlong confrontation with the vested interests that have surrounded these monopolies for generations. Often these interests will seek to shelter behind the national governments that either own or protect them. Arguments will be used – on safety, consumer protection, or security of supply, for example – to suggest that the interests of competition and efficiency should for once take a back seat. Thus one part of the problem is that there is indeed a potential conflict between the application of competition rules to utilities and other legitimate policy objectives. Can we afford to abandon long-nursed concerns about security of supply in energy, for example, just for the sake of introducing competition? Is environmental protection not a more important aim of energy and transport policy than competition? Do not regional or social considerations have to be taken into account in telecommunications policy so as to ensure that people living in remote areas are connected to the system? In short, the argument runs, utilities are not just by their nature unsuited to competition; they are too important to be left to the market. That is why most of them are controlled by the state and even those which are not, basically in Britain, remain heavily regulated.

Yet the savings that could be gained from allowing free, or at least freer, play to market forces are considerable. Most businesses spend large amounts of money on basic utilities such as electricity and telecommunications. Increased European competition would force the utilities to become more efficient. Resource allocation would improve and there would be increased trade, all of which would lead to lower costs. Charges to consumers could be reduced and the benefits would spread rapidly into the rest of the economy. Although a considerable amount of guesswork must be involved in making such predictions, the Commission has claimed that a single market in energy would yield economic gains worth at least Ecu 16bn a year, or 0.5 per cent of Community GDP.[1] The single market in energy reaches further than simply putting an end to national monopolies in electricity and gas, but this figure is something of an indication of the scale of potential savings in this area. It does not include the further substantial gains that would be derived from separate moves to liberalize equipment procurement in the energy sector. For telecommunications, the Commission has suggested that the savings generated by implementing the proposals contained in its 1987 Green Paper would amount to as much as Ecu 10bn.[2]

The different national regimes applied to utilities in Europe also distort competition across a broad front. Pricing policies adopted by utilities matter because they affect the basic conditions under which industry operates. And they vary widely.

One example is the different charges applied by the various European telecommunications concerns. In general, the pattern has been that long-distance calls cross-subsidize local calls, but there are some striking differentials between member countries. In 1986, according to the Commission, connection charges ranged from a low of Ecu 31 in West Germany to a high of Ecu 235 in Ireland. Similarly, the prices charged by utilities to certain customers may involve a covert subsidy. In recent times, Electricité de France (EDF) has attracted the attention of the Commission's competition authorities because of the special deals it has offered to selected large users. This led first to an investigation into an arrangement between EDF and Pechiney, the leading aluminium producer, as a result of which EDF was forced to raise its price. More recently, the Commission has also opened an inquiry into a proposal by EDF to offer advantageous rates to Exxon Chemicals, which is planning to make a FFr 2.6bn new plant investment in Normandy.

Meanwhile, the fragmentation of utility services into separate national markets means that standards are not always compatible. Loading gauges differ on railways, for example. A frequently cited argument for opening up the market in telecommunications is that a quarter of data traffic sent across European frontiers fails to reach its destination because networks do not interconnect properly. All this is a broad impediment to the development of a true European market.

Although there is thus a clear case for a market-orientated European approach to regulating utilities, such a policy has to be tailored to fit in with other objectives. It has to take account of the extent to which the utilities are in fact national monopolies. By way of introduction, this chapter begins with an outline look at developments in three representative sectors: telecommunications, the energy utilities (electricity and gas), and transport. This is necessary because there is little interdisciplinary expertise across the spectrum of utilities and because it should reveal a pattern to the Commission's approach about which some general conclusions can be drawn.

The experience in telecommunications, the energy utilities and transport

The move to liberalize European utilities has gone furthest in telecommunications. This is not surprising, since telecommunications is a sector subject to a particularly rapid pace of technological change. It is also generally recognized to be a key industry of the future and one on which Europe will depend for its future growth and prosperity. In preparing its 1987 Green Paper, the Commission calculated that the market in telecommunications services, which turned over Ecu 75bn in 1987, will more than double in relative importance by the turn of the century. Its share of Community GDP will rise to 7 per cent from roughly 3 per cent at present.

None the less, it was not until 1987 that serious debate about telecommunications and the single market finally got under way with the publication by the Commission of its Green Paper.[3] This set out a programme of liberalization going far beyond that contemplated or adopted in most member states. The only area in which national authorities were to be allowed to retain their monopoly rights was in the provision of basic network voice telephone services and telex. Their regulatory roles were to be separated from their operating roles. The supply of terminal equipment was to be liberalized, as were so-called value-added services like electronic mail and video-text, as well as the small but rapidly growing market in data transmission. Technical rules were to be drawn up to ensure free access to the networks, and a European Telecommunications Standards Institute was to be established to harmonize standards across the Community. Although the Green Paper was vague in many of its proposals, it set the agenda for a debate on reform that was to continue for the next two years.

This combination of measures was designed to introduce competition into the industry, while recognizing that part of it remained a natural monopoly. Although the development of mobile phone networks is now starting to challenge this assumption with increasing insistence, the industry is still dependent on a fixed network of wires to deliver the services it provides. In the United Kingdom, Mercury, the second provider of telecommunications services, has created an alternative network connecting major cities. But it does not reach into the remoter rural areas and Mercury still depends on being able to interconnect with British Telecom to provide a full service to its customers. For the time being, it would be absurdly expensive to duplicate networks in such a way as to ensure the universal provision of service, even in rural areas, so the Green Paper envisaged that natural monopolies would be allowed to continue. Their rights would, however, extend only to the provision of a basic telephone service, which, the Commission calculates, generates 90 per cent of their revenue. Competition would be introduced both where equipment is attached and in the use to which the network can be put. The separation of the regulatory role of the telecommunications authority from its operation role was a logical corollary of this. Given that some degree of operational monopoly was to continue, it was deemed necessary to ensure fair play.

As if these proposals were not controversial enough in themselves, they have also led to a bruising battle between the Commission and the member states over the way in which they have been forced through. Early in 1988, the Commission launched a plan to liberalize the market in telecommunications equipment such as modems, PBX private exchanges, and second and subsequent telephones. The proposal was drawn up without consulting member states and relied on the little-used Article 90 of the EEC Treaty for its legal basis.* With certain exemptions, Article 90 subjects state enterprises to the competition rules set out elsewhere in the Treaty. In particular it can be used against public enterprises to make them subject to the rules on economic concentrations in Articles 85 and 86. The Commission's claim to use it unilaterally as the backing for what many saw as the imposition of a new policy infuriated member states. The content of the directive itself was not particularly controversial, but the idea that the Commission could override sovereign powers in this way was regarded as so dangerous that it was quickly challenged in the European Court by France, with the backing of West Germany, Belgium, Greece and Italy. After agonizing for many months, the United Kingdom decided not to participate in this action because it regarded it as more important to get the right solution for the industry.

---

*More detailed discussion on the pivotal role of Article 90 follows later in this chapter. The full text appears in Appendix I.

Without waiting for a decision by the Court, the Commission used Article 90 to weigh in with another directive at the turn of 1988-9. This time the subject matter was telecommunications services, and several member states objected because the proposal included liberalization of data transmission. France, for example, had invested heavily in converting its system to Integrated Services Digital Network (ISDN), which allows voice or data to be transmitted more efficiently along existing cables. It argued that data transmission should be part of the basic telecommunications monopoly on the grounds that it was an essential service. Like several other member states, it felt that the profits from data transmission, which were needed to cover such loss-making activities as services to rural areas, would be creamed off by private operators from the United States, such as GEIS (General Electric Information Services) and EDS (Electronic Data Systems). Although basic telephony provides 90 per cent of telecommunications revenues currently, its growth is likely to be slower in future than that of data communications. Without data communications revenues, the monopoly authorities would have less opportunity to cross-subsidize their services. Another fear was that liberalization of the market in data transmission would pave the way for the expansion in telecommunications of the US computer giant IBM.

In contrast to these two directives, the Commission decided not to use Article 90 to launch the next plank of its reform programme, the Open Network Provision (ONP), which lays down harmonized standards and rules requiring the basic network to be accessible to would-be providers of telecommunications services. This is seen as a crucial part of the package because it seeks to ensure that member states will not hide behind spurious standard requirements to discriminate against the new competition or to hamper it in other ways, for example by providing only low-quality lines.

The Commission argued that there was an important distinction between its first two directives and the ONP. The directives were designed to enforce rules already set out in the Treaty but never implemented; they did not involve new policy. The ONP, by contrast, did involve the creation of new policy and therefore should be subject to consultation by member states. The Commission sees this distinction as being one of legal importance.

57

The idea that the two directives did not involve new policy is the basis of its defence in the European Court of its use of Article 90 to underpin them. There is, however, a practical issue at stake as well. In the first instance, the complex rules set out in the ONP would have to be enforced by member states themselves. Such rules could not easily be written without the collaboration of those same member states. Since the ONP is an integral part of the reform, a first conclusion from the telecommunications experience has to be that liberalization could not succeed by relying on Article 90 alone.

In the event, the Commission and the member states did not wait until the Court had ruled on the use of Article 90 before reaching a compromise on the services directive and the ONP. Late in 1989 the member states reluctantly agreed to liberalize the market in data transmission from January 1993 in return for the right to license new operators. Less developed states – basically Portugal, Greece and Spain – will be allowed until 1996 to comply. The Commission is entitled to vet the licensing schemes to make sure they conform to European competition rules. Any conditions they contain must be transparent and non-discriminatory. The market in other value-added services was to be liberalized from April 1990, while, to prevent it becoming a bureaucratic barrier to the development of competition, the ONP was to be voluntary rather than compulsory, with the Commission retaining the reserve power to enforce ONP conditions if it felt the voluntary approach had failed to lead to a proper connection between the Community's networks.[4] The agreement covered only a framework ONP, leaving detailed directives to be agreed later.

Like telecommunications, energy utilities were left untouched by the original single-market proposals published by the Commission in 1985. One problem is that these utilities constitute particularly deeply entrenched national monopolies. Technically they are less amenable to competition than telecommunications, where the basic network can be the basis for a whole range of different services. Since the oil shock of 1973, moreover, the Commission's entire policy in the energy field had been dominated by security-of-supply considerations. It was difficult to abandon this priority for the sake of competition. Any policy designed to introduce competition into the energy field, meanwhile, has to take account of environmental factors, while it is also almost certain to offend vested interests with long-standing political pull, such as the West German coal-mining industry. For all these reasons, the Commission has proceeded more cautiously on the energy front. Its initiatives have come later than those in telecommunications; there has been no recourse to the draconian measures of Article 90; and they are more gradual and piecemeal in nature.

What finally pushed the Commission into action was a growing conflict between France and Germany. While EDF has surplus power at its disposal as a result of its successful investment in nuclear capacity, electricity prices are high in Germany, where the power industry is forced to buy expensive domestic coal and pass on the cost to consumers through a special tax known as the *Kohlepfennig*. France would like to offload some of its surplus electricity in the German market, but cannot because of the barriers to cross-border trade that have been erected to sustain the high prices resulting from the *Kohlepfennig*. The French government claims that German coal is unfairly subsidized. The German government argues that the French nuclear programme was also subsidized (although subsidization is very hard to prove). The debate is further complicated by growing public suspicion of nuclear power in most of Europe and by the need to deal with the social consequences of steering the German coal industry through a period of long-term decline. This has been exacerbated recently by environmental worry concerning the burning of fossil fuels.

EDF would also like to sell its cheap energy to Portugal, but Spain, which currently supplies its neighbour's generators with coal, is resisting opening up its grid for this purpose. This is subsidiary to the Franco-German issue, however, which is generally seen as the key challenge for the Commission in regulating the energy utilities. To an important extent, the success or failure of its policy will depend on how this problem is dealt with.

There are four main strands to the Commission's approach. It has been seeking agreement from member states that would require transparency in prices charged to large industrial users of gas and electricity. Similarly, it would like early mandatory reporting of large new investment proposals in the energy field. Third, it is anxious to develop cross-border trade in electricity and gas, a move which is linked to the *Kohlepfennig* problem. Finally, the Commission has been exploring the possibility of opening up the gas and electricity grids across Europe to all third parties. This is sometimes known as 'common carriage', although a more appropriate description would be 'open access'.*

Even the simplest parts of this plan, which involve price transparency and investment notification, have turned out to be controversial. The Commission's intention in seeking mandatory early notification of investment plans was simply to improve the flow of information and avoid duplication of effort. Its plan did not foresee any actual controls at European level on new energy investment. Yet several member states have complained that the scheme risks leading to leakage of confidential and sensitive details of proposed investments. Similarly, commercial confidence was cited by a number of countries as grounds for objecting to price transparency. At the end of October 1989, member states did, however, agree the outlines of a scheme that will involve utilities in reporting twice-yearly to the Commission on prices charged to large customers. The Commission will subsequently publish average prices. Once implemented, the scheme will bring the arrangements for utilities closer to those applied to coal, where price-reporting is mandatory and the results public. The new transparency, however, will apply only to downstream prices affecting residential and commercial users. The Commission has evaded the issue of upstream transparency. The prices that producers receive are highly opaque and the industry has gone to great lengths to ensure that this remains the case.

One consequence of greater price transparency should be an increase in pressure for the opening-up of cross-border trade. Trade in coal and electricity amounts to less than 5 per cent of total European consumption. Market distortions, such as those prevailing between Germany and France, would be impossible to maintain if there were open trade between the two countries. This would reinforce legal efforts by the Commission to deal with the

---

*The term 'common carriage' has a particular technical significance in the gas industry. It is used to describe a rule whereby anybody who insists on using pipeline capacity is allowed to do so even if existing users are forced to reduce their share of that capacity on a pro-rata basis. The so-called 'common carriage' feature of Britain's gas industry legislation is in fact an open-access rule, providing for capacity to be made available to all-comers on a first come, first served, basis.

Kohlepfennig problem. It has declared its intention of attacking this arrangement as an abuse of the Treaty's competition rules. In theory it should be possible for it to do so using a combination of Articles 90 and 85, which deal with restrictive price arrangements. In practice, its task would be much easier if member states were prepared to facilitate cross-border trade.

Opponents of this plan sometimes argue that the logical conclusion of such a policy might be a situation where France became a dominant supplier to the rest of Europe because its cheap power would squeeze out other producers. Security of supply would then be threatened, with serious economic consequences if something went wrong with one of its nuclear power stations or its systems failed in other ways. The theoretical rewards, on the other hand, are twofold. First, increased cross-border trade would reduce the need for costly surplus generating capacity to be maintained at the national level to cover power failures. This would generate large savings, which could be passed on to consumers. Second, there ought to be an immediate effect on prices, and costly producers would have to learn quickly to become more efficient.

In practice these rewards may be rather elusive. It is still psychologically difficult for power industries operating at a national level in Europe to regard reserve power abroad as secure. National security considerations are bound to arise and they will be difficult to overcome. Meanwhile, the reaction time for any power-generating concern seeking to become more efficient is slow. Normally this will require expensive investment in new plant. Resistance to cross-border trade, which forced speedy change in supply patterns, is thus likely to be very great. Subsidized or not, the problem with France's nuclear programme is, ironically, that it has been too successful and has turned its industry into a serious potential threat to other European utilities.

One conclusion at this stage is that national insistence on security of supply will remain an obstacle to the introduction of competition in the energy field. Another problem is that competition which led to lower prices and increased consumption would inevitably raise questions about the environment. Given the growing public concern in this area, it is hard to see how the environment can fail to complicate the task of regulators, and this may well prove a serious impediment to the development of competition.

Although cross-border trade in gas is better developed than that in electricity, the idea of European arrangements to facilitate trade are still regarded as controversial. West Germany's role as a conduit for the import of Soviet gas means that some of the infrastructure already exists for common carriage, but Germany is reluctant to give up its sovereign control in this area, as is the Netherlands as a supplier (the United Kingdom is not yet hooked up to the European system). The idea of opening up transit rights between one country and another is seen as the thin end of the wedge, which would lead eventually to full common carriage in which all-comers would be able to demand a share in the pipeline capacity, even if that meant squeezing the share of existing users.

Some have argued that common carriage in Europe would stimulate greater use of natural gas in power generation, a development that would certainly have positive environmental repercussions. Others warn that it might jeopardize the long-term supply agreements which have been negotiated with third countries, notably Norway, Algeria and the Soviet Union, on which Europe depends for about a third of its supply. For all these reasons, common carriage could not come about without appropriate regulatory arrangements at the European level. Without a European regulatory body in place, there is little prospect of full-scale liberalization. The United Kingdom provided for limited open access to gas pipelines as long ago as 1982, and strengthened this provision considerably in 1986, when it privatized British Gas. It has accompanied this with the creation of an independent supervisory authority in the form of Ofgas, but nowhere else in Europe is there a similar separate body. With such limited precedent at the national level, it is unlikely that member states will allow an independent regulatory authority to be set up at supranational level.

In electricity there are still some technical doubts about the feasibility of common carriage, but the industry tends to overstate these. It is vehemently opposed, not least because it fears that consumers would gain such a wide freedom of choice that the market would become uncertain and unpredictable. Power generation is an activity demanding very large investments with long pay-back periods. Such investment might simply cease to be viable.

Despite a European Court ruling in 1985 that the Community's failure to agree a common transport policy was a breach of the Treaty of Rome, progress in the transport area has also been slow. So far, most effort has been concentrated on the areas of road haulage, shipping and aviation. Late in 1989 member states agreed for the first time to allow cabotage in road haulage. Cabotage is the business of picking up traffic in a foreign country and transporting it to a destination within that same country. It has proved extremely difficult for the Commission to persuade member states to agree to air transport liberalization that would produce cheaper fares. But airlines and road haulage do not pose the same natural monopoly problem that we have so far been discussing. More relevant in this context are airports (where no reforms are under way) and rail transport. Although its plan has yet to be considered seriously by member states, rail transport is an area in which the Commission has in fact produced reform proposals. Here again, the essence of its plan, launched late last year, lies in splitting off from the rest those parts of the business that are amenable to competition.

As a first step, member states would have to account separately for that part of the business engaged in providing the infrastructure and that part which actually provides the service. It is in the provision of service that competition is seen as possible. Community transit rights would have to be allowed for international rail companies. In practical terms this would help create the basis for an international network of high-speed trains, although the national rail authorities do not regard such a change in the rules as a prerequisite for such a service. The changes would clearly pave the way for new rail companies eventually to enter the market in competition with national ones. A similar idea has been considered as one possible basis for the privatization of rail in the United Kingdom. It would also require agreement on harmonized standards. Ultimately, according to one European official, it opens up a distinction similar to that between national airports and the airlines which operate through them.[5] Standards are, however, a major problem for rail. Different loading gauges mean, for example, that continental trains could not enjoy free access to the UK network even after the opening of the Channel tunnel; British bridges and tunnels are simply too low.

Finally, a mention must be made at this point of public procurement. Legally this is not regarded as part of competition policy and is handled by the Commission's Directorate General responsible for industrial affairs. None the less liberalization of public procurement will have a profound effect on the behaviour of utilities and holds out scope for considerable cost savings. The Community has long had rules requiring open procurement in public works and supplies. As part of the single-market programme, liberalization is also to be extended to the so-called 'excluded sectors' of water, energy, transport and telecommunications. Liberalization in these areas is also under discussion in the Uruguay Round of the GATT.

In late February 1990, member states agreed on a new directive for the excluded sectors, but an indication of the caution with which some of them view liberalization is that the directive specifically excluded the supply of energy itself. This was to prevent France acquiring a right to sell its electricity anywhere it chose in Europe. The United Kingdom also managed to secure agreement on the terms under which its oil and gas exploration industry might be exempted. A further controversial point is that the directive included a clause giving preference to European producers. Buyers would be allowed to dismiss bids with less than 50 per cent European content, but, if they agreed to accept such a bid, it would have to carry a price at least 3 per cent below the lowest EC bid in order to win the contract.

This aspect of the directive will be discussed in greater detail in Chapter 5, which deals with trade policy. It is worth noting here, however, that the insertion of such a clause militates against the development of competition within the utilities themselves. One of the advantages enjoyed by the new independent utilities, such as Mercury in telecommunications, is precisely that they have no established links with national suppliers and are free to shop around the world for the best possible equipment. This is clearly a factor which helps them compete. Although the 'Buy Europe' provision is regarded as simply a negotiating lever in the Uruguay Round, it could carry a considerable anti-competitive effect.

One of the principal problems remains, however, that of compliance and enforcement. This is to be the subject of a separate later directive which had not been put forward at the time of writing. Ownership of utilities in the Community ranges from fully private, through mixed, to fully state-owned. Privately owned utilities argued that they were responsible to shareholders, and not to governments, for their procurement policy. Procurement rules would impose unfair compliance costs on them, they claimed. British Gas estimated that the cost of compliance would be as much as £24m a year. State-owned utilities, on the other hand, have proved reluctant to see their counterparts exempted from the general rules.

The quest for a suitable compliance procedure has had to take these problems into account. As a result, the main element of the system that the Community is expected to propose is a regular audit, which would throw up patterns of preferential procurement. This bad behaviour could be dealt with by the Commission, but it could also form the basis for a damages claim by the injured party. The costs of compliance through audit would be relatively low for a company with good management control of purchasing, but there is still a problem with delays in dealing with infringements. By the time the courts had reached a verdict on a procurement case, the damage would have been done because the plaintiff would have lost the contract in question and might have suffered a serious commercial setback as a result. One possible approach to this might be to adapt a practice from Belgian law which would allow a national court, on the basis of a preliminary finding, to order that an infringement be corrected. The finding would be accompanied by a threat of serious punitive damages if, in a subsequent full hearing, the allegation of infringement was upheld and it had remained uncorrected.

Almost any compliance scheme in this area will meanwhile have the drawback of relying on individual firms to complain. The compliance mechanism for public works and supplies agreed by member states also puts heavy emphasis on complaint by injured firms and has been widely criticized. The fear is that firms which suffer injury will be reluctant to fight back because they are often heavily dependent on public contracts. To challenge a contract award would thus be to bite the hand that feeds them.

The strategic approach to the procurement debate adopted by companies so far has generally been to organize themselves to establish a position inside national foreign markets. Thus, for example, Britain's GEC (General Electricity Company) has developed a heavy engineering link with CGE-Alsthom, and the Swiss-Swedish ABB (Asea Brown Boveri) concern has acquired BREL, the former British Rail Engineering Ltd. This suggests that, whatever the eventual outcome of the debate in Brussels, procurement markets will, for the time being, continue in practice to be organized along national lines. But there are some signs of change. For example, Siemens and ABB have both won contracts in the UK power sector. Also, the French construction company Bouygues created a stir in 1989 when it successfully complained that Denmark had infringed the rules on public works in awarding the contract for its Great Belt Bridge. This had specified the use of local materials and labour. The contract was not suspended, but Bouygues won the right to seek damages and recover its bidding costs.

Commission officials believe that the publicity surrounding such cases will encourage others. Ultimately firms will come to realize that the prospect of winning business in other Community countries is not as forlorn as they thought. This change in mentality will eventually open up the market, but it is impossible to legislate for and will take a long time to materialize.

Conclusions

It is now possible to draw some general conclusions from the experience of telecommunications, energy and transport.

In all three sectors it has proved difficult to address the core monopolies at the heart of the system, although reform has gone furthest in telecommunications, where the core monopoly is weakest. Because of this, the approach has tended to be one of vertical disintegration in which the activities of the utilities have been unbundled and competition applied to those areas which are amenable to it. Thus in telecommunications the approach has been to distinguish between running the basic network and the provision of services. In the energy utilities the aim is to treat separately the function of production from that of distribution. In rail transport it has been recognized that the network would remain a monopoly even though it could be used by several competing companies.

This approach appears to acknowledge a limit to which competition can be introduced into the utility area. However, the continuing existence of core monopolies raises a number of regulatory problems. How far should they be allowed to compete in other areas of the business, such as the provision of value-added networks in telecommunications? How should they be compensated for the loss-making services they are obliged to provide for social reasons? How can they be made to open up the network on a non-discriminatory basis to other potential players in the market? This all calls for complicated regulatory machinery, which, in the long run, will probably be most effective if it operates at the European, rather than the national, level.

Regulators will also have to be flexible enough not to become hooked on the idea that their sole task is to control a monopoly. It was noted above that various technological developments in telecommunications are likely to challenge the network monopolies in the not too distant future. Further down the road is also the possibility that superconductivity in electricity will undermine the monopolies of the present grid systems. Admittedly it is hard to see the network monopoly being challenged in water supply, but it is important for the regulators to take account of technological change that might switch the emphasis of their work away from regulating a core monopoly, to providing for free competition.

For the time being, however, even the vertical disintegration approach adopted by the Commission has turned out to be a delicate task, since the various Articles of the Treaty leave considerable rights with member states concerning the management of state-owned monopoly utilities, running, in transport, even to subsidization (see Articles 37, 77, 90 and 222 in Appendix I). A piecemeal approach has therefore had to be employed which relies heavily on the collaboration of member states. These are often reluctant to offer such collaboration because they are prey to strong vested interests demanding the maintenance of the status quo.

Moreover, the political momentum in favour of liberalization is limited because, at least in the initial stage, the main beneficiaries would be major firms rather than the public. The broader public may perceive considerable benefit in the prospect of cheaper air fares, but, as was noted earlier, the whole question of airline deregulation involves a different set of considerations because airlines do not involve natural monopolies as the utilities do. In a debate on liberalizing the utilities, the public is frequently more aware of the potential risks in terms of, say, conflict with environmental concerns, or the provision of services to remote areas, or the loss of jobs in national champion industries. The

Commission has therefore had to approach its task without a broad-based constituency of public support in member states.

Much of the conceptual thinking behind the Commission's approach is drawn from the UK experience, where deregulation and privatization of utilities have gone furthest. Thus, the United Kingdom has provided, although so far ineffectually, for open access in gas and is now doing so in electricity; its privatized electricity generators will be allowed to sell power directly to large consumers; and it has introduced a substantial degree of competition into its telecommunications industry, where the monopoly of British Telecom, the former state-owned telecommunications authority, has been broken. Britain's success in dealing with its problems goes hand in hand with its privatization programme, but, although privatization may help foster a climate favourable to the development of competition, it is not an answer in itself.

This is clear from the UK experience in the water sector, where privatization has opened the door to the purchase of UK water companies by French concerns. This may be economically beneficial, since the mere threat of being taken over will keep any management on its toes, but it does not mean that the monopoly has been broken and that true competition has been introduced.

At the European level, the Commission has no power to dictate that utilities should be privately owned. Article 222 of the EEC Treaty allows member states to choose how their ownership will be organized. Elsewhere, experience shows that competition does not flow automatically from private ownership. Hong Kong and Germany have a long tradition of private ownership in the utilities sector, but no tradition of domestic competition.

The key to developing competition lies in regulation. Even the United Kingdom has had to accompany its privatization programme with some complex and artificial arrangements to ensure competition; for example by creating two power-generating entities, which have involved extensive regulation. The real challenge for the Commission lies in this area. Although the scope is clearly there for it to create some improvement, the chances of full success in bringing competition to the utility sector are slim in anything other than the very long term.

Even the regulatory control mechanisms that are open to the Commission in other areas may be difficult to apply to the utilities.

For example, not only are transport subsidies commonly accepted by policy-makers, but Article 77 specifically permits subsidization in this sector. Elsewhere it can be difficult to prove. Although West Germany has argued that French electricity is cheap because the nuclear programme of EDF has been subsidized with cheap capital provided by the state, EDF in fact raises its own funds on international capital markets and, with only one or two exceptions, has borrowed without a formal French state guarantee since 1973. Technically, therefore, it is raising funds without government support, even though investors may choose to regard state backing as implicit. Thus the inquiry into its deal with Pechiney, which led eventually to an increase in the price charged to the aluminium concern, was based on the notion that it was abusing a dominant position (which is in breach of Article 86) rather than any accusation of unfair subsidy. To a very large degree, the Commission is forced to rely on persuading and cajoling member states to agree to new directives, using the approach laid down in Article 100a of the EEC Treaty. This is, for example, the case with the liberalization of public procurement. The weakness of such an approach is that sometimes member states will balk at even the simplest of suggestions (such as notification of energy prices) or water down the efficacy of a proposal (by making it difficult to enforce open public procurement). This helps explain why the scorecard to date shows only limited signs of success.

Even though the Commission is now working hard to reform the energy sector, for example, the most likely short-run effect is that the volume of cross-border trade will increase. This would in itself be no bad thing. Were EDF able to sell its cheap electricity to West Germany, industry there would benefit from lower costs. There is a distinction to be made here between cross-border trade among utilities, and cross-border trade involving sales direct to consumers in the foreign country. The latter would have a much more immediate effect on prices and competition. Were it to be allowed in Germany, it could become the catalyst for competition in the domestic market, where there are already several generating companies.

However, Germany is a special case in this regard, and the notion that utility companies in one country could compete with those in another is a far cry from the introduction of competition at all levels. The only sector in which any real degree of competition has been introduced is telecommunications. As noted above, however, this was possible partly because technological change was fostering a more competitive environment anyway. Even so, the traditional authorities managed to hang onto their monopoly over basic telephony, and the change that was achieved was made ultimately possible only by means of the Commission's decision to use Article 90 to force reform on member states. It is to an analysis of this controversial action that this chapter now turns.

Article 90 bans the application of measures that infringe EC competition rules to any public undertaking or to any undertaking which benefits from special or exclusive rights. The Commission is entrusted with the power to ensure that its provisions are applied. It, the Article states, 'shall, where necessary, address appropriate directives or decisions to member states'. The Commission's defence of its use of Article 90 in the telecommunications equipment and services directives rests on this clause. It says it was simply carrying out its responsibility for ensuring that the provisions of the Article were met. No new policy was involved. The issue of a directive was appropriate because the alternative was a cumbersome procedure of taking a series of individual cases to the European Court of Justice.

However, the French case seeks to undermine this position. It says that the wording of the Article does not ban the extension of special and exclusive rights (such as those controlling the use of telecommunications terminal equipment). Indeed it is worded in a way which suggests that they are permitted. The Commission failed to show that the exclusive rights had been used in any illegal manner and should have demonstrated this on a case-by-case basis. That it failed to do so suggests that it was attempting to do more than simply fulfil its obligations of surveillance and enforcement. It was trying to introduce a new set of regulations for an entire economic sector. Article 90 is not designed to serve this purpose and, even though Article 90 does provide expressly for directives, such a step should have been undertaken through recourse to Article 100a of the Treaty, which requires consultation with member states.

At the time of writing, the Court had still to pronounce on the case, although in February 1990 Mr Giuseppe Tesauro, the Advocate General, had delivered a preliminary opinion which found against the Commission. At the heart of the legal debate is the question of how the competition rules can be made to apply in a situation where special and exclusive rights have been conferred on utilities under the terms of Article 90. Although the Article subjects such utilities to the rules of competition contained elsewhere in the Treaty, Mr Tesauro took the view that a point-by-point verification of the way the exclusive rights were established and operated was needed before the Treaty could be shown to have been infringed. Such a conclusion could not be reached in the abstract. It had to have a concrete basis. This therefore effectively ruled out Article 90 as the basis for the telecommunications directives, which were supposed to prevent unspecified actual and potential infringements of the competition rules. There is no obligation on the full Court to follow the Advocate General's opinion. Frequently its judgments are different, and Mr Tesauro's opinion did not mean that the Commission's case was lost. None the less, it threw into stark relief the risk to the Commission's strategy if the backing of Article 90 were withdrawn.

It was argued above that the Commission's efforts to bring competition into the utility sector would not get very far without collaboration from member states. It is also true, however, that this collaboration is only likely to be forthcoming if there is a degree of pressure involved as well. The use of Article 90 has provided precisely such an instrument of pressure in reforming telecommunications. Without it there is some doubt whether the more controversial reforms would successfully get off the ground at all. The equipment directive which provoked France's recourse to the European Court has now been ratified and implemented by member states and cannot be undone. It will be recalled that it was the manner of pushing through the directive, and the precedent this set, that prompted the Court action, rather than the content of the directive itself. The services directive is a different matter. This was a reluctant compromise by member states who generally wanted to keep data transmission as part of the national monopoly. If Article 90 had not been involved, there is some doubt as to whether it would have been possible to reach this compromise, and some in the industry fear it could unravel if the Court's final ruling goes against the Commission.

The conclusion has to be that a negative Article 90 ruling would deal a serious blow to the already fairly limited prospects of introducing competition into the utility sector in Europe. This conclusion applies to all the utilities, not just the telecommunications sector, in which Article 90 has been used.

Responsiveness of member states to pressure for change in other areas may have been increased by the use of Article 90 in telecommunications. It will certainly become a much greater factor if the Court rules in favour of the Commission. Without such an instrument, the Commission's case is considerably weakened. There is nothing else in its armoury which could substitute for the role that has been attributed to Article 90. Of course Article 90 could still be used in specific individual cases, but this would be cumbersome and time-consuming. Other than that, the Commission would be thrown back on external pressure, mostly from the United States, as a catalyst for change. Although this is strong in telecommunications, it is inconceivable that it could ever be significant in rail transport. Where pressure was applied by Washington, it might also be counterproductive. Member states could be all the more tempted to dig in their heels as a matter of national pride and Community solidarity.

One further point needs to be made about regulating the utilities, although it would become rather theoretical if the Court's decision went against the Commission. The regulatory process is all the more complex because it involves an attempt to create competition in markets where previously it has simply not existed. It has already been seen how anxious the telecommunications authorities were to preserve profits from activities such as data transmission, which they said were necessary to pay for loss-making parts of the service to rural areas. In one sense the reason why they are being allowed to retain a monopoly reflects the need to provide certain services universally, even where they are uneconomic. The regulatory authorities have to take this point into account, but they also have to regulate in such a way as to encourage competition. The basic idea behind the ONP in telecommunications was to respond to this by creating a level playing-field, under which standards were to be harmonized and access to the network guaranteed. This may not, however, be adequate to secure competition. The reasons are much the same as those for which the Commission itself has argued in a different context: that national treatment alone may not be enough to secure for European banks a proper foothold in the Japanese market.

In banking, the Commission has argued that simply treating European banks in the same way as Japanese ones will not give them effective access to the market, because general interest-rate regulations, for example, would prevent them from developing a customer base by bidding aggressively for deposits. What is needed is a regulatory field tilted somewhat in favour of the new entrant. Otherwise he is liable to remain effectively excluded. Given the inertia of consumers of utility services, and the network of relationships which the incumbent monopolies have developed over the years with their suppliers and customers, competition may need to be given a little extra shove so that new entrants to the market can build up the critical mass that makes them serious players.

Sir Bryan Carsberg, head of Oftel, the United Kingdom's independent telecommunications regulatory agency, has drawn attention to this problem in a domestic UK context. In an interview with *The Financial Times*, he said that competition would not develop unless Oftel took steps to favour the new players.[6] That is why the requirements on Mercury to provide a universal service were less onerous than those on British Telecom. Mercury will have to assume more social obligations once it becomes better established. One of Oftel's tasks is to decide when this time has come. A similar argument applies to cable television companies, which are allowed to provide telephone services over their network, whereas British Telecom may not transmit television pictures. 'What we are doing is giving the others a bit of a time advantage, a head start', said Sir Bryan.

A separate but related issue involves the setting of standards. Harmonized standards are an important prerequisite for market-opening because they ensure that one part of the network can be connected to another. They therefore create sure conditions for new entrants seeking to enter the market. Yet there is a delicate balance to be struck in setting them. Harmonized standards that simply replicate those already applied by one or more existing large suppliers will give them a head start, making it harder for newcomers to establish themselves. A completely new set of standards will force these same suppliers to adapt. Initially, at any rate, this could push up their costs, reducing the overall benefits from the introduction of competition.

These problems call for a powerful combination of skill diplomacy, determination and independence on the part of the regulatory authorities. It is arguable that such strengths do not necessarily reside in the Commission. The task of providing oversight to ensure fair competition does not necessarily fit easily with that of actually formulating policy. For this reason, the United Kingdom decided to separate the two functions and create Oftel, which is independent of the Department of Trade and Industry, where policy is formulated. Many believe that a similar approach is also needed in Europe.

This applies not just in telecommunications, but in other areas as well. Commenting on the prospects for competition in gas, a recent study by the Royal Institute of International Affairs and the University of Sussex noted that the ready availability of large reserves of natural gas in countries that export to the EC had created the right conditions for the emergence of competition. There was a great obstacle, however, in the reluctance of those who own the transmission systems to relinquish any part of their control. The promotion of greater competition, the study concluded, 'almost certainly requires the establishment of a European regulatory authority, with powers to require technical and commercial information and establish transparent transmission tariffs'.[7]

It would be unrealistic to assume, however, that such European regulatory institutions could take on all the day-to-day functions now being carried out by regulators at the national level. Their function would have to be largely confined to supervising the national regulators, who should promote transparency and should ensure that provisions agreed within the Community for the introduction of competition into the utilities sector were being respected in practice. Even for them to be able to assume this relatively limited role, it would be necessary for a framework to be agreed setting out their powers of intervention and the basic rules that they would have to apply. The risk of negotiating such a framework too early in the process of utility liberalization would be that it would incorporate a lowest-common-denominator effect, setting limits to the obligations of member states and discouraging further progress towards competition. From this point of view, the best time to create such institutions would be after all the elements of the liberalization process have been agreed by the Commission and the member states together. Independent regulatory institutions may then be needed to ensure that rules on competition are effectively applied. Their effectiveness depends, however, on the rule-book being correct in the first place. They cannot substitute for the need to develop the right regulations.

A further difficulty with the creation of such institutions is that, if they are to have their own legal powers, they require a change of the EEC Treaty by unanimity. Even if the Commission were anxious to cede its own power in this regulatory area (which it is not), the problem with persuading member states to agree is that it cannot be contemplated in the present, rather fluid, situation, where detailed policy is still being worked out.

This is an unsatisfactory conclusion to reach insofar as industrial standards are already being set and, once established, they will be difficult to alter. Since in practice the creation of independent supervisory bodies is not an option, the competition authorities in Brussels will have to work hard to fill the gap. On them lies the special burden of quickly building up expertise and resources in these areas and of using them to make sure that the hard-won gains of liberalization are not lost through backsliding in the writing and implementation of the fine-print legislation.

Notes

1 *The Internal Energy Market*, Commission of the European Communities, Brussels, May 1988.
2 *Common Market for Telecommunications Service and Equipment*, Commission of the European Communities, Brussels, June 1987.
3 Hugo Dixon, *The Financial Times*, 11 December 1989.
4 Tim Dickson, *The Financial Times*, 23 November 1989.
5 Ibid.
6 Interview with Hugo Dixon, 5 February 1990.
7 *A Single European Market in Energy*, joint report of the Energy and Environment Programme, Royal Institute of International Affairs, London, and Science Policy Research Unit, University of Sussex, 1989.

5

THE TRADE POLICY CONNECTION

Peter Montagnon

Officially there is very little that links competition policy and trade policy. Although it is creeping into some of the new areas being discussed in the Uruguay Round, competition policy falls outside the remit of the GATT.* In the Community, as in most national governments around the world, responsibility for the two falls on different shoulders. Both are, however, areas in which the Commission itself has considerable powers of discretion. The main thrust of this chapter is to argue that much more coordination is necessary to ensure that competition and trade policy are mutually supporting. The links between the two are close, but what is not clear is whether the Community recognizes this in its institutional arrangements.

It is self-evident that an open attitude to trade will reinforce a policy designed to foster competition in domestic markets. One danger in the 1992 context, however, is that the industrial restructuring provoked by opening up Europe's internal markets may prove so painful that industry will be tempted to seek external

---

*Among other things, the Uruguay Round is considering liberalization of trade in services and better protection for the intellectual property. Both have competition policy implications. The former requires non-discriminatory right of establishment by service companies in foreign national markets; an aspect of the latter is restrictive business practices related to the transfer of technology.

protection. The idea of a trade-off between strong domestic competition policy and a protectionist external trade policy has a natural attraction for industry. The combination would allow industries to develop within Europe the critical mass claimed to be needed to take on world markets.

Yet experience has shown that, once granted, such external protection rarely proves temporary. It provides industry with an excuse to delay adjustment. Underlying the increased attention being paid to competition policy in the Community is the realization that competition will play an important role in promoting the adjustment needed to secure the efficiency gains promised by the single market. A protectionist trade policy that softened these adjustment pressures would thus be counter-productive. It would dilute the gains promised from increased internal competition, while there would also be a heavy cost in terms of damaged trade relations and export markets lost through retaliation.

In its public statements on this issue, the Commission has been at pains to deny that its intention is to build a fortress around European industry. However, the risk is not that this will happen in any explicit way. It is more likely to occur by default. For this reason it is necessary to look more closely at the subtle ways in which trade policy can affect competition. This chapter begins with dumping, where the Commission has already been accused by some of abusing its rights under GATT to such an extent that it has begun to operate an unofficial industrial policy. It moves on to subsidies and countervailing duties, including the trade policy issues raised by Airbus support. From there it continues to a discussion of the use of 'reciprocity' conditions to force an opening of the markets of other countries. Finally, it looks at some of the direct external implications of competition policy decisions, particularly with regard to Community relations with the European Free Trade Association (EFTA). Its main conclusion is that the institutional framework in which trade policy is developed by the Commission will need to be altered. At present, trade policy and competition policy can easily pull in different directions. More transparency is needed, and more thought should be given to the impact that trade policy can have on domestic competition.

Dumping and subsidies

In a speech to Norwegian industrialists early in 1990, Sir Leon Brittan, EC Competition Policy Commissioner, argued that anti-dumping measures were 'a legitimate and internationally agreed trade-policy instrument to cope with market distortion and unfair competition'. Despite suggestions that the EC should eschew such actions against members of EFTA as part of the conditions needed to create the European Economic Space (EES), he said the Community would be obliged to maintain the right to employ anti-dumping measures until such time as 'truly equal or analogous rules of competition' had been established between the two blocs.[1]

This view of anti-dumping highlights the connection between trade and competition policy. Dumping occurs when a firm from one country sells in the markets of another goods priced below cost or below their price in the home market. This is held to have a predatory effect. For it to be successful in squeezing out producers in the importing country, however, certain conditions normally have to be fulfilled in the exporting market. First, it has to benefit from external protection so that goods sold cheaply abroad are not simply re-exported back to their place of origin. Second, in most cases the exporter has to be dominant in his home market. Otherwise the removal of mainly foreign competition will avail little. In practice, it is internationally accepted that dumping may be countervailed whether or not the conditions for predation are fulfilled. It is only necessary to prove that goods are being sold at dumped prices and that this causes injury.

Thus it is frequently argued that anti-dumping actions would not be necessary in a world in which strict competition policy was uniformly applied. Anti-dumping duties are not applied on trade within the Community. Here the problems of predatory activity are dealt with by Directorate General IV (DGIV), which is responsible for competition policy. Anti-dumping actions are the responsibility of Directorate General I (DGI), which is responsible for trade policy. Ostensibly, at least, the purpose of anti-dumping actions is to help ensure fair competition in the Community's markets. This chapter will argue, however, that they have actually had the opposite effect. They discriminate against foreign firms by making it hard for them to penetrate the EC market and they have also encouraged cartels within Europe.

There is one important technical difference in approach

between anti-dumping and domestic competition policy as it affects predatory pricing. Although some Community countries, such as France, have national laws which prevent domestic companies from selling in the national market at prices below cost, this is generally permitted at the European level, as is discount-pricing in specific market segments. The result is that European competition policy permits new entrants to break into the market by pricing their products as 'loss leaders'. The idea is that 'loss leaders' can be permitted because the cost of using predatory pricing to establish an actual dominant position on the domestic market is very great. Companies will rarely, if ever, do so unless the market is protected in other ways. Recourse, however, by a foreign firm to promotional prices that were lower than those on his home market would render it vulnerable to charges of dumping and the imposition of duties. In practice, therefore, the use of anti-dumping measures can discriminate against foreigners, making it more difficult for them than it is for indigenous firms to gain access to the market. In such circumstances the imposition of anti-dumping duties is likely to impede something that normal competition policy would allow. In short, while anti-dumping measures may be justified as preventing predation, they actually go much further and wider than that.

In the interest of maintaining strong competition on the domestic market, there is thus a case for ensuring that anti-dumping measures are subject to strict discipline. Unfortunately, this is not what happens in the Community, where the administration of dumping policy is in the hands of a special division within DGI that deals with trade matters. This division has to follow an elaborate set of rules, but it is entrusted with all the tasks related to the imposition of duties. It has to determine whether dumping has actually occurred, and whether European industry has suffered injury as a result, and calculate the appropriate level of duties, bearing in mind the general interest of the Community. In doing so it may balance the interest of industry against the short-run effect on consumers of the higher prices that would result from duties.

Admittedly the final outcome of this process has to be approved by the Council of Ministers, but this is normally a perfunctory process during which little detailed analysis is made of the Commission's calculations. Those who feel mistreated by the

79

process can take the matter up with the European Court of Justice. Defenders of European anti-dumping policy often claim that the Court has found no fault with it. Yet the Court's business is not to make qualitative judgments about policy. It is simply to establish whether the correct procedures have been followed.

Another aspect of European anti-dumping policy that is relevant to competition is the frequency with which it results in price undertakings. One recent example of this was the agreement at the end of 1989 between the Commission and several Japanese companies that established a floor price for D-Rams as a means of resolving an earlier dumping action. Although details of such agreements are never published and are negotiated individually with each exporting firm, they are frequently criticized because they transfer extra profit to the exporters and create what is in effect a cartel. Some trade officials in Europe believe that price undertakings also help promote anti-competitive behaviour by firms in the importing country. Certainly they help by establishing a guaranteed market price which quickly becomes the norm. Even though an *ad valorem* duty is more flexible than a fixed floor price, and does not reward the dumping exporters, it also provides a price shelter to European firms. Such a price shelter might be doubly useful to any European firms intent on creating a cartel. Not only does it remove the obstacle created by foreign competition; but it does so with the approval of DGI, providing a shield against concern being shown by DGIV.

It is not surprising, therefore, that there is evidence of a connection between anti-dumping actions and cartel behaviour by European companies. In its annual report for 1988, the UK Office of Fair Trading highlighted one case involving soda ash producers. Mr Patrick Messerlin, Professor of Economics at the Institut d'Etudes Politiques de Paris and a consultant to the World Bank, has also drawn attention to the problem. A case similar to that of soda ash had occurred with polyethylene and polyvinyl chloride after dumping duties were imposed in the early 1980s, he notes.[2] In fact, about a quarter of all the cartel cases initiated by the Commission since 1980 concern firms and products that have also been involved in anti-dumping cases. They represent about a quarter of all anti-dumping cases. One further point noted by Mr Messerlin is that anti-dumping actions are very lucrative for the firms concerned. The polyethylene and polyvinyl chloride duties allowed prices in Europe to rise by 11 and 14 per cent respectively, generating additional annual revenues of Ecu 352m and Ecu 312m respectively for EC firms. This was roughly ten times the cartel fines eventually levied by the Commission.

It follows from this that any serious effort by the Commission to maintain a competitive environment in its domestic market needs to entail a fresh look at dumping. Ways should be found to ensure that dumping action is taken only against genuine cases of predation. One way of limiting the number of cases might be to redefine dumping as occurring only when a foreign firm is selling below cost in Europe, although this formulation would be tighter than the generally accepted international definition. Another way might be to rewrite the rules for calculating dumping margins so that they are no longer tilted in favour of a positive finding. Here the Uruguay Round could help by providing clear international guidance on permissible practice in calculating margins. Finally, dumping provides a clear example of why DGIV should, in addition to its responsibility for competition, take a close interest in the formulation and practice of trade policy. This point will be developed further in the conclusion of this chapter, in the discussion of possible institutional change. Dumping is not, however, the only area in which there are close links between trade and competition policy. Another is subsidies.

By comparison with anti-dumping, the Community makes very sparing use of countervailing duties against products benefiting from unfair subsidies paid in third countries. One reason for this is that, unlike their US counterparts, European officials consider it hard to prove that a subsidy has been granted which has a direct affect on trade. Another is that subsidies are relatively uncommon in those parts of the world, such as the Far East, that have been the source of Europe's most serious recent trading problems. A third reason, and probably the most important, is the fear of drawing fire on Europe's own subsidies, not only in agriculture, but in manufacturing as well. The Community's submission to the Uruguay Round discussion on subsidies in 1989 was ambivalent, not least because it sought specifically to leave the door open to Airbus support, as well as arguing a general case for the social value of subsidies.

This is not surprising, since Airbus subsidies occupy a special place in European thinking on industrial support. Airbus Industrie is the only venture of its kind in the Community. It is competing in the market for large civil aircraft, and the two other firms in this market are both in the United States. It is therefore difficult to make out a case against them under Community law, which defines as illegal only subsidies that distort trade and competition within the Community. Moreover, any attempt to pursue such a case would be fraught with political difficulty, since Airbus is recognized to be not only a project of considerable European importance, but one that brings benefit to a large number of member states.

In fact it would be inconsistent of the Commission to leave Airbus subsidies off the list of aids that are to be reined in in connection with the single market. Although they do not involve a direct distortion of trade within the Community, they do distort competition indirectly because they benefit the individual companies that make up the Airbus consortium. The competition authorities in Brussels thus have a considerable interest in the outcome of the trade dispute that has developed between Europe and the United States as a result of these subsidies.

The Airbus issue is important not only in its own right, but also because it is symptomatic of a wider issue that is now starting to come to the fore in international trade policy. This is the question of the degree to which governments should support, either with subsidies or through a relaxation of their normal rules on restrictive practices, industry's efforts to make the technological breakthrough to develop products of a world class. Another relevant product is high-definition television, where success depends not only on companies combining to afford large-scale investment in R&D, but also on the collaboration of governments in setting appropriate standards. Conflicts in this area over the next few years are likely to become the sharp end of trade policy. The GATT is ill-equipped to deal with them, but they can almost certainly be resolved only by international collaboration to establish reasonable rules of engagement. Competition authorities will need to play an important role in developing such collaboration.

Another area in the field of subsidies in which the distinction between trade policy and competition policy has become very blurred is the discussion on steel. This has intensified since the decision taken by the United States in 1989 to continue its voluntary restraint arrangements in steel until 1992.

In exchange for an agreement to renew its steel quotas for only two and a half years instead of the normal five, the United States sought a series of bilateral agreements from its trading partners requiring them to limit their own steel subsidies. It was not difficult for the EC to agree to this side of the bargain because it was already imposing a regime so strict that the US negotiators were surprised when they were shown it. The end-result was a consensus for market-access restrictions on both sides to disappear by March 1992, coupled with discipline on subsidies, market access and dispute settlement. It has been suggested that the aim should be to multilateralize this agreement in the Uruguay Round, possibly extending it to products other than steel. The chances of converting such an arrangement into more general rules for subsidies are slim: the problem with such agreements in the GATT is that they tend to be weaker than the strictest internal disciplines. In the case of steel, the chances of achieving a strict multilateral discipline are rather higher because of the bilateral arrangements that the United States has agreed with other producers. The existence of such a multilateral agreement could reinforce competition policy in the steel sector. It would make it harder for member states to seek, and be granted, a derogation from internal disciplines.

This principle can apply in other areas, too. Some international trade officials consider that the Commission has been helped in its efforts to liberalize the European telecommunications market by external pressure from the United States. Its ability to maintain the liberalization process will clearly also be affected by what is agreed for telecommunications at the multilateral level. If the European Court rules against the use of Article 90 as a liberalizing tool, external pressure may be the only effective means left of promoting change. The competition authorities in Brussels, who have been behind efforts to bring about liberalization in European telecommunications, thus have an interest in a strict agreement emerging from the Uruguay Round. Once again, there is a case for their becoming actively involved in trade policy.

The institutional problems raised by this will be discussed later. First, however, it is necessary to consider the debate on reciprocity as it relates to competition policy.

The great reciprocity debate

In many of the measures that it has taken to implement its 1992 single-market programme, the Community is moving ahead of the rest of the world. This is particularly true of the services sector, where it is creating liberalized markets with opportunities for outsiders that do not exist in many countries elsewhere. It is also true of public procurement. Not surprisingly, many in Europe argue that the benefits of the single market should not be extended to companies from countries that are not similarly open, and that the Community should use its own liberalization to force open the markets of others. The idea of writing a European preference into the latest public-procurement rules, for example, is to provide the Community with leverage in the Uruguay Round.

Such a reciprocal approach is different from the way reciprocity works in the GATT, however. Reciprocity in the GATT involves a balancing of concessions, not an attempt to produce exactly the same conditions in every market. The GATT negotiating process also allows multi-sectoral reciprocity; it does not restrict bargains to one sector. Bargains that are struck are then 'bound' so that the parties concerned are held to them. They are also obliged to apply the concession to all, on a non-discriminatory basis. The essential point about this process is that it creates a momentum towards liberalization without worrying particularly what the status quo is at the outset, or what the specific outcome is, provided the move is in the right direction.

In the services sector, however, and to a large extent in public procurement, GATT disciplines do not apply. The targeted bilateral approach to liberalization adopted by Europe in these areas implies a very different approach. It is beneficial to competition only if it works, however, and the risks that it will fail to open up the markets of Japan, East Asia and the United States are considerable. By sticking to its guns in those circumstances, the Community could cut itself off from the outside world. Foreigners would be denied access to European markets if their markets were not fully open to European firms. These, in turn, would be denied access to foreign markets in retaliation. One of the problems is that, in most of the instances in which reciprocity arguments have arisen, there are as yet no international rules defining just how far governments can go. Also, here again, competition would suffer because the number of foreign participants in the market would be limited.

The first formal precedent in this area was set by the Community in its second banking directive in the spring of 1989. Article 7 of this directive provides for the Commission to examine how Community banks are treated in third countries. Where it is found that a foreign country is granting 'effective market access and competitive opportunities comparable to those accorded by the Community to credit institutions of that third country' the Commission may seek a mandate from the Council of Ministers to negotiate comparable access for European banks. No mention of sanctions is made in this part of the Article, but the directive goes on to say that new banking licences may be withheld from institutions coming from countries where 'credit institutions of the Community do not enjoy national treatment and the same competitive opportunities as domestic credit institutions'. This is substantially milder than many had originally feared, given some high-level suggestions in the Commission that reciprocity meant requiring European conditions to be fully matched in foreign markets and that sanctions should include the right to withdraw licences from banks already operating inside the Community.

A similar debate took place over the merger control regulation, where the point at issue was the right of European concerns to acquire companies in third countries. The 1988 bid by Nestlé of Switzerland for Rowntree, Britain's York-based confectioner, provoked an outcry from British industry, which considered that it should be disallowed because the Swiss market structure, with its division between registered and bearer shares, prevented British companies from buying Swiss firms. The arguments on this issue are complicated by the fact that a level playing-field scarcely exists in the Community: some countries, such as the Netherlands, maintain an effective system of barriers to foreign takeovers, while Britain is the most open. This is clearly a deterrent to competition within the Community, since it sets limits to market access. It is particularly important in some sectors, such as retail banking, in which market access can be gained only by merging with, or taking over, a firm with an established local reputation. None the less, the fact that there were internal problems within the Community on this point did not stop pressure building up for a reciprocity clause within the merger regulation.

On the surface, the wording of the resulting Article 24 of the merger regulation seems innocuous. Once again it allows the Commission to seek a mandate to negotiate comparable treatment for Community firms when it appears that 'a non-member country does not grant Community undertakings treatment comparable to that granted by the Community to undertakings from that non-member country'. There is no provision for sanctions, and it would seem that only minimal pressure can be applied.

By comparison with some national instruments, including the reciprocity provisions of the United Kingdom's Financial Services Act (which gave birth to the European debate on this issue), the language of Article 24 is very mild. But the operation of this clause depends on how it is handled by the Commission, which is bound to come under severe pressure from time to time to use its right to seek a mandate for negotiating conditions of better access for European firms in third-country markets. Since it is not empowered to threaten sanctions, the stance it will take in these negotiations might seem to be very weak. In practice, however, this need not necessarily be the case, since such access negotiations will rarely be taking place in isolation.

Negotiations may involve an EFTA country, such as Switzerland, in which case they will be just one item on a long agenda of issues, most of which will involve Switzerland as a 'demandeur'. Or take Japan, for instance. At any one time there are a number of issues at stake between the EC and Japan. At the time of writing these include the application of EC dumping rules to Japanese products, local-content requirements and rules of origin. All of them are related to Japan's perceived need to improve the access of its firms to the European market. In practice, therefore, it may matter little that the Commission is not able to impose sanctions against countries which discriminate against EC investors. There will usually be a possibility of linking this negotiation to something else, and of threatening, indirectly, to impose sanctions by denying a concession that the other side is seeking. This is a temptation which a Commission concerned with maintaining open, competitive markets will have to resist. Failure to do so might lead to a general increase in the level of protectionism, which might be even worse than a regulation that had permitted sanctions. The reason is that the origin of the increased protection would be obscure.

Another controversial area involving reciprocity relates to public procurement. Part of the single-market programme involves, as was seen in Chapter 4, the opening-up of procurement in the hitherto excluded sectors of energy, telecommunications, transport and water. The potential efficiency gains could be large, and the liberalization of procurement is an integral part of the Commission's effort to bring greater competition into the utilities sector. None the less, the Community has been anxious to avoid frittering away its bargaining power in the Uruguay Round before any multilateral agreement is struck on public procurement. There is also genuine resentment in Europe against the 'Buy America' legislation and against the deeply nationalistic Japanese approach to the award of government contracts.

Written into the new rules for the liberalization of European procurement in the previously excluded sectors of energy, telecommunications, transport and water is a provision calling for European preference where bid prices differ by 3 per cent or less. Even though this is modest compared with the discrimination practised elsewhere, it is almost certainly in breach of the central GATT principle that countries should not discriminate against imports. The Community has stated that this provision will be removed only if the Uruguay Round leads to a satisfactory general agreement on procurement in the excluded sectors, a prospect that has to be regarded as, at best, uncertain. There is thus a good possibility that European preference will be a lasting feature of the new procurement regime and that this will lead to some serious international trade rows.

To be fully effective, however, the procurement rules need to avoid discriminating against any third-country suppliers. If the compliance arrangements turn out to be weak, as suggested in Chapter 4, such specific discrimination against foreign suppliers would further reduce their bite. Conversely, foreign participation would become increasingly important in preserving competition in the European market if the directive were to succeed in producing the desired rationalization in the supplier industries. The process is expected to lead to economies of scale and cost savings that could be passed onto consumers. Although it is difficult to forecast with any precision, some estimates developed in connection with the Commission's 'cost of non-Europe' study have suggested a reduction in the number of telephone-switching companies from eleven to two, and in the number of locomotive manufacturers from the current sixteen to three or four. Only four or five boiler makers would remain.[3]

Commission officials argue that these numbers would be sufficient to ensure effective competition on the European market, with or without foreign competition. Within Europe, however, a network of links is developing between the main suppliers. This is moving in the direction of an oligopoly of suppliers at European level, replacing those that have hitherto operated at national level. The secure admission of foreign suppliers to the market would help ensure a broad range of choice for purchasers and make the rules more effective. Above all, it would put downward pressure on prices.

Finally, the European preference scheme has engendered a further potential problem in the form of a local-content provision. Purchasers will be allowed to refuse preference to any bids with less than 50 per cent European content. This is likely to lead to some fierce arguments, not only within Europe, but also internationally. Rules on content and origin are difficult to apply objectively, as is shown by the European argument with the United States and Japan on printed circuit boards. In some areas, it may prove difficult to define what 50 per cent European really means. This applies especially in the high-technology area of telecommunications, where equipment often carries a high level of imported components.

Competition policy and the outside world

So far this chapter has argued that there is a close link between the operation of trade policy and policy towards competition in its broadest sense. It must also be recalled, however, that even the execution of a more narrowly defined competition policy has increasing external implications. This is shown both by the European proposal for a treaty with the United States on competition matters, and by the high profile that competition policy has assumed in the Community's discussion with EFTA on the creation of the EES.

One consequence of heightened European Commission activity in the field of merger control could be its involvement in vetting mergers involving firms in third countries, particularly the United States, that happen to have a large turnover inside the

Community. The risk is that this may lead to a conflict with the US anti-trust authorities, and to uncertainty over rights of jurisdiction. This was the rationale behind Sir Leon Brittan's proposal in April 1990 for a treaty between the two countries. He suggested that such a treaty would provide for exchange of information, lay down detailed procedures for consultations and provide for independent arbitration of disputes.

Once again, this is symptomatic of a wider problem, namely that commercial disputes between countries no longer involve matters related to trade merely in physical goods. Increasingly they are concerned with the way in which policy towards industry and investment is conducted in an age of mobile capital flows and rapid technology advance. As with the Airbus issue already discussed, these problems call for closer international collaboration in the competition policy field. Closer to home, however, the EC/EFTA discussions on economic cooperation show just how difficult harmonization actually is to achieve.

There are two main problems in these discussions as they affect competition policy. The first is the extent to which EFTA countries can adopt rules created by the European Community in connection with the single market if they have no say in the formulation of those rules. The second problem relates to the way in which these rules can be enforced to the satisfaction of the European Community when it cannot claim jurisdiction in EFTA markets without undermining the sovereignty of governments in those countries. Yet, without what Sir Leon Brittan called 'truly equal or analogous rules of competition', it will be difficult to exempt EFTA countries from EC trade-policy actions.[4] Although Sir Leon was referring specifically to anti-dumping actions, his remark is also true of countervailing duty measures against subsidies, which are of equal, if not greater, importance in the debate.

Although many of the EFTA countries have been prepared to go along with the EC rules in the competition area, this remains a problem for Switzerland, which both is fiercely jealous of its sovereignty and lacks a strong competition-policy tradition. Sweden, together with Norway and Finland, does not actually prohibit cartels unless they are shown to be contrary to the public interest. Like the other EFTA countries, except Switzerland, these nations have been willing to adapt their policy towards cartels and bring it in line with that of the Community. Austria takes the view that such harmonization is a logical consequence of its application for membership. This, however, still leaves the question of enforcement. One suggestion from the Community has been that its rules would simply be enforced inside EFTA by the DGIV in Brussels.

The issue of subsidies is more complicated. Since 1988, EFTA has itself been paying closer attention to this area by requiring notification of state aids. The EFTA Secretariat, however, is ill-equipped to scrutinize such notifications and bring abuses to book. Decisions on whether abuse has occurred are left to EFTA's Council of Ministers, acting by consensus. To make the EFTA system compatible with that of the EC thus requires large-scale institutional change. One proposal from the officials concerned (which had not been adopted at the political level when this chapter was written) was to increase the Secretariat's power of surveillance and to establish a penal system for inquiring into allegations of abuse. The adoption of its verdicts would be subject to majority vote in the EFTA Council, and there would be a mechanism for ensuring that subsidies found to be illegal were rapid.

That such an approach could even be considered shows that there is substantial willingness on the part of EFTA to take a pragmatic approach towards the general need to harmonize its competition rules with those of the EC. But there is also a limit to the extent to which some EFTA countries are prepared to see their sovereignty infringed, and there is also, on the EC side, a lingering suspicion that EFTA's own enforcement mechanisms would not be strong enough to match those of the Community. In practice, harmonization of competition policy between the two blocs may well not go far enough to ensure the exemption of EFTA countries from EC trade-policy measures in the fields of dumping and countervailing duties. It is worth recalling that Canada failed to achieve an exemption from Washington's trade-remedy laws in its free-trade talks with the United States, although a special system of bi-national dispute panels was established to mitigate the effects of any friction. Trade policymakers still guard their rights in the areas of dumping and countervailing duties very jealously.

The need for institutional change

It has been argued so far that the EC competition authorities need to pay close attention to trade policy. Even when its intentions appear to be benign, trade policy can easily produce results that thwart the objectives of competition policy. This is true in the old traditional areas, such as dumping and subsidies, and also in the newer trade-policy areas, like services and investment, where demands for reciprocity in regulating market access have engendered a new form of protectionism. Ultimately, however, it is market access that is at stake in both competition and trade policy. To be effective the two should pull together. Let us now consider what institutional changes might be introduced at the European level to help ensure that this is what actually happens.

As long ago as 1984, the OECD produced a report on the interaction of trade and competition policy.[5] This recommended that governments should subject their trade-policy decisions to a checklist of questions on their likely impact in areas such as prices, the availability of choice to consumers, structural adjustment prospects and investment flows. Subsequently, the OECD followed up its report with a study on the effects of trade barriers on the automotive industry in four selected countries: the United States, Canada, France and the United Kingdom. This found that the effect had been costly in competition terms: 'Concentration has generally increased, competition has been reduced, and the danger of widespread collusion has been enhanced.'[6]

Admittedly, laws against unfair trade practices, such as dumping, were specifically excluded from the trade measures that the OECD thought should be subject to its checklist. There is no reason, however, why questions should not be asked openly on the impact of all trade-policy decisions, including anti-dumping actions, both on consumers and on domestic competition. The more openly such questions are discussed, the less likely it becomes that trade policy will come into conflict with the needs of domestic competition policy. What is needed is a way of formalizing this process in Europe.

One possibility might be to follow the Australian example and set up a special body with an independent mandate to calculate and publicize the economic cost of the support that industry receives. This has been the role of the Australian Industries Assistance Commission, and will continue to be so, although it is currently being revamped and rechristened the Industries Commission. It is an independent statutory body, operating through the public inquiry process, which provides advice to the government on structural adjustment and micro-economic reform matters. Traditionally, the Australian government has sought the Commission's advice before making decisions affecting support for industries. It is not, however, obliged to accept that advice. In a submission to GATT in 1989, the Australian government said: 'The public enquiry process has assisted community understanding of the costs of assistance in the manufacturing and agricultural sectors and of impediments in all sectors of the economy.'[7]

Although no comparable effort is made in Europe either to achieve such a high degree of transparency or to solicit a wide range of public views, it would be easy to reject such an approach on the grounds that Australian policy is still surprisingly protectionist. Yet without the Industries Commission, the Australian economy might be a good deal less open. It is a resource-based economy with a small domestic market for manufactured goods. This is a combination that makes the pressure of protection unusually strong.

Unlike the proposal for a European Cartel Office, which was discussed in Chapter 2, the creation of such a body to investigate and publish appraisals of trade-policy proposals would not require an amendment to the Treaty. It would none the less be regarded as a radical departure from the present approach. Whereas the idea of a European Cartel Office is modelled on the present German system, no European country has any institution similar to the Australian Industries Commission. The chances of it receiving much political impulse from member states are rather small. So are the chances of the Commission throwing its weight behind the creation of an institution whose published advice would be a real constraint on its freedom of action.

Here the United States can provide some useful pointers. One difference in its approach to the implementation of trade policy compared with that of Europe, is that the task is shared between several different institutions. In anti-dumping cases, for example, the Commerce Department is responsible for determining whether dumping has occurred, while the degree of injury to the domestic industry is assessed by the International Trade Commission (ITC). This is an independent body whose members are appointed by the

Administration, but on long-term mandates, which means that they are less likely to be swayed by short-term political considerations. There is already a difference here from European practice, where the responsibility for finding dumping and injury rests, as noted earlier, with the same division of DGI. The difference goes further. The injury tests conducted by the ITC are based on public inquiry. One of the organizations which can, and does, make its opinion known during the inquiry process is the Federal Trade Commission, which, together with the anti-trust division of the Justice Department, is responsible for domestic competition policy. This link does not exist in the same way in Europe. Although European trade-policy decisions are subject to collective scrutiny by the entire Commission as well as member states, this process is, as noted, cursory in the case of anti-dumping actions. There is no formal requirement for DGIV to make its views known, even though the result of such actions could undermine the objectives of competition policy.

As with Australia, it would be possible to argue at this stage that the United States provides a bad model. The United States has resorted more freely, over a longer period, to anti-dumping and countervailing duties than the EC. This in no way impairs the case in favour of the EC adopting greater transparency. The focus of recent complaint has been the unilateralism that has been written into US trade law, not necessarily the administration of its remedy procedures for trade. Indeed, in its implementation, US trade policy is remarkably transparent and, given the extreme pressure to which both the Reagan and the Bush administrations have been subjected as a result of the trade deficit, this has probably helped limit the current slide into protectionism.

The key lies with transparency. Here it is worth pausing to consider another example from Australia's experience. In 1988, in addition to the Industries Commission, Australia created an Anti-Dumping Authority to give advice on whether dumping or countervailing duties should be imposed in response to specific complaints. The guidelines under which the authority operates require it to have regard to the government's intention that anti-dumping and countervailing mechanisms should not be used as a substitute means of providing assistance to industry, or to shield it from the need to adjust to changing economic circumstances. Crucial to its charter is the requirement that the authority advertise inquiries, invite submissions from the public and publish its findings. As Figure 5.1 shows, the number of anti-dumping actions initiated by Australia plummeted at the time the authority was created.

Figure 5.1   Australian anti-dumping actions 1982/3 to 1988/9

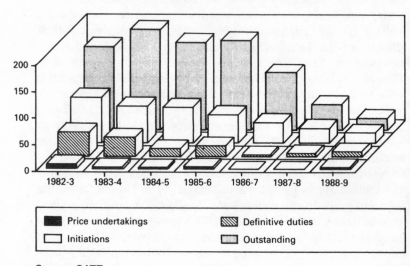

Source: GATT.

Taken together, the Australian and US approaches to anti-dumping and countervailing duty measures suggest that two changes could be introduced by the EC to help ensure that such actions do not harm competition or go against the interests of consumers. First, the task of proving that dumping has occurred and that of assessing injury could be assigned to separate parts of the Commission. Second, transparency could be improved. These two measures would help ensure that dumping duties are applied only where genuine predation has occurred.

A sensible solution would be to assign to DGIV the responsibility for conducting the injury test in cases of anti-dumping and countervailing duty actions. It is, after all, already engaged in the business of determining whether internal subsidies distort trade and competition within the Community. Its expertise in the nature and impact of unfair competition would certainly be appropriate to assessing injury as a result of dumping.

At one level, such a change would yield the simple advantage that the task of dealing with dumping would be split in two. Outside influence would be brought to bear on the powerful division of DGI, which has, up to now, held tight sway over anti-dumping procedures. This would also, however, create a useful dialectic between two parts of the Commission whose background and priorities mean that they would approach the same problem from different angles. DGI is concerned with trade, and does not bother itself with competition. DGIV is concerned with competition and, as has been shown, needs to concern itself with trade as well. To develop interaction between the two would put both on their mettle. The quality of argumentation, and with it the quality of decision-making, could be expected to improve.

The idea that DGIV could become responsible for injury-testing in trade remedy cases is bound to be controversial, particularly since the Community traditionally levies dumping margins related to the scale of injury, rather than to the actual level of dumping. DGI would be ceding considerable power to DGIV by this arrangement. It would therefore be fiercely resisted by those member states which view anti-dumping as a legitimate weapon for curbing the unfair trade practices of Japan and other East Asian countries.

There remains, however, a less radical possibility by which DGIV could become more closely involved in trade-policy decisions. It has the additional advantage that it would help ensure that these did not conflict with the objectives of competition policy.

The idea would be that each time DGI was considering an anti-dumping action or other protective measure, it would be required formally to solicit the views of DGIV concerning the likely effect of such a measure on competition within the common market. DGIV would not be empowered to veto such a measure, but its opinion would be made public to give added transparency to the decision-making process. As part of its submission, DGIV would be expected to assess the cost that the proposed action would impose on consumers. In negotiations leading up to the D-Ram price undertaking with Japan in 1989, European users of memory chips complained vehemently that their interests were being sacrificed to those of the chip producers. They said their costs would rise as a result of the measure and that this would affect their ability to compete in world markets. The Commission argued that it had done its best to take user interests into account; but such statements rest for their credibility on the good faith of those that make them. Under the change proposed here, user interests would have to be considered, and the public would be made aware of the arguments involved. Its responsibilities make DGIV a natural advocate for competition and consumer interests in the Community. Experience has shown that there is a need for such an advocacy role, which would replicate the checks and balances built into the US system.

Of course, it would not always be possible to predict with certainty what the effect of a given trade-policy action on domestic competition would be. The role of DGIV would be more to assess the risks than to forecast what would actually happen. It is clear that the risks to competition are greater if protection is being granted to a domestic industry that is already heavily concentrated. The chemical industry cases cited earlier would fit into this picture. The risk of competition on the domestic market being impaired would also be greater if there were few alternative sources of imports to that which was being accused of dumping. To take two actual examples, dumping duties imposed on foreign manufacturers of photograph albums might be anti-competitive because there is already very little internal competition in this sector in the Community. Duties imposed against imports of denim cloth from a particular source might have less of an impact on competition because there are several international sources of supply. Account would have to be taken of the possibility of other exporters raising their prices as a consequence of any dumping duties being imposed. Bearing such factors in mind, it should be possible for DGIV to quantify the risks to competition. Its report could then be taken into account in calculating the level of any dumping duties that were actually imposed, although these would still actually be decided by DGI.

This approach still does not take account of the problem that it is precisely in situations where the domestic market is already heavily concentrated, and where there are few sources of imports, that the risk of predation is greatest. DGI is geared up to consider this risk above all. It does not have to justify its actions on the grounds of their effect on competition. The public involvement of DGIV in the decision-making process would thus help balance the activity of DGI in three separate ways. First, it could result in greater reluctance among firms to seek trade protection. Second, in cases where protection was granted to a heavily concentrated industry through the imposition of dumping duties, such duties might turn out lower. DGI would have to justify them against the backdrop of a negative report on the competition implications from DGIV. Third, such a report would serve as a signal to the companies concerned that their future activities were likely to be closely scrutinized for signs of collusion. Fines imposed on companies found guilty of operating a cartel after the imposition of dumping duties should be sharply increased from their present level, which is inadequate as a deterrent.

This would be a relatively modest change, but one which should have a significant effect not only in preventing cartels, but also in ensuring that the overall cost to the consumer is taken into account when trade remedy measures are considered. At present, consideration paid to the consumer on such occasions is perfunctory. A transparent system that drew attention to the cost of protection would doubtless raise questions in many cases about whether it constituted a price worth paying to remedy the alleged injury sustained by the producer seeking support. In this way it would prevent the erection of fortress walls around Europe after 1992. Any member state which denies that this is the intention of the single market would have little intellectual justification for opposing the suggestion that has been made here.

Notes

1 Speech to the Norwegian Confederation of Industries, Oslo, 29 January 1990.

2 Patrick Messerlin, *Anti-dumping Regulations or Procartel Laws: the EC Chemical cases*. World Bank, International Economics Department, 1989. See also *The Financial Times*, 28 February 1990.

3 Paolo Cecchini, *The European Challenge, 1992: the Benefits of a Single Market*, Commission of the European Communities, Brussels, 1988.

4 See reference in note 1 to speech in Oslo, 29 January 1990.

5 *Competition and Trade Policies: their Interaction*, OECD, Paris, 1984.

6 *The Costs of Restricting Imports: the Automobile Industry*, OECD, Paris, 1987.
7 'GATT Trade Policy Review Mechanism: Australia', mimeo, GATT, Geneva, 1989.

6
CONCLUSION

Peter Montagnon

It is clear from this examination of developments in European competition policy that the Commission is now acquiring additional discretion as a result of the single-market programme. Indeed, it is desirable that it should do so, if national governments are not to thwart the objectives of the single market by using their powers in the field of competition policy to protect their own champion industries.

Thus the new merger-control regulation gives the Commission exclusive power to vet larger mergers. Subject to the decision by the European Court on its use of Article 90 to enforce reform, the Commission is also exercising a new, and central, role in the regulation of monopoly utilities. In this area, too, it will have new responsibilities for enforcing open public-procurement policies by member states. Even in areas, such as subsidies, where the Commission has traditionally enjoyed a large degree of discretion, it is busy reviewing its powers in an attempt to make them more effective.

Yet many problems still remain. The merger regulation provides for only the largest takeovers to be vetted by the Commission; it is still also open to different interpretations concerning the degree to which mergers should be judged solely on a competition yardstick; member states have proved resistant to even the simplest reforms designed to bring transparency into the electricity and gas markets; even with a much tighter policy it will be difficult for the Commission to impose discipline on R&D subsidies or on those for large projects, such as Airbus. Finally, trade policy, an area in which the Commission also enjoys considerable powers of its own, can easily pull against competition policy, producing a contradictory effect that encourages cartels and limits the open market.

A first general conclusion is therefore that, despite the lip-service now being paid across the Community to the importance of competition policy, member states still retain considerable powers to pursue their own industrial policies. A second is that, even at a European level, there is a risk that competition policy could be put to one side when it is seen to conflict with other objectives, such as regional development or European technological progress. This is not to suggest that such priorities can easily gain the upper hand, especially given the very strict approach adopted by DGIV under its present Commissioner, Sir Leon Brittan. But it is necessary to look beyond the tenure of one single Commissioner. A different personality at the helm could produce a distinct change in emphasis. The pressures on the Commission are intense, as is shown by the difficulty experienced by Sir Leon in persuading his colleagues to subject the Air France purchase of UTA to European merger control early in 1990. Without a strong Commissioner in charge of competition policy, the risk is that industrial considerations might begin to dominate. Further institutional change is needed to prevent such backsliding and to ensure that the free play of competition is permanently established as a guiding force in European economic policy.

For what is true at a national level also applies to the Community as a whole; governments almost invariably lack the skill and the judgment to choose industrial winners. In Europe, after 1992, the temptation to look for winners at Community level will be very strong. The lessons of the past suggest that to succumb to this would be a mistake. Professor F.M. Scherer of Harvard University has argued that some of the leading companies that escaped US anti-trust action in the early days – such as US Steel, American Can and International Harvester – have atrophied, disappeared or abandoned their traditional lines of endeavour.[1] Many brewing companies which expanded through mergers have performed less well than those, such as Anheuser-Busch and Miller, that grew by cultivating their own brands.

According to Professor John Kay of the London Business School, the liberalization of intra-European trade may lead naturally, in some sectors, to greater consumer choice, rather than to the availability of a more restricted range of cheaper goods at lower prices and produced by a smaller number of larger firms. Professor Kay argues that this is particularly true for sectors, such as processed food and drink, in which consumer preferences for product diversity are strong, but he argues that it is also true for cars, a sector which many expect to be subject to intensive rationalization. There are few industries in which mergers between large established producers are an appropriate response to 1992, he says. 'The larger relative size of American and Japanese companies in many sectors, particularly electricals and engineering, is the result of their greater success, not the cause of it.' Such success has almost never been founded on the suppression of competition in their domestic markets, he adds.[2]

It would thus be a mistake for the Commission to try to steer industry towards the creation of large units, which can benefit from the single market and, in so doing, strengthen their international competitiveness. It is the market, not the governments or the Commission, that should determine the response of industry towards 1992 and be in the position of picking the winners. The best, indeed the only, way of ensuring that this is what actually happens is to orientate competition policy towards competition and away from other public interests. Professor Scherer has also pointed out that this is in itself a difficult task.[3] The impact of a given merger transaction on competition will be assessed differently, depending on how the market is defined. Whereas the Continental Can case of 1972 dealt only with the market for metal containers, US cases have looked at metal containers plus glass bottles plus plastic containers. If the market is defined too narrowly, mergers that pose no threat to competition could be disallowed. If it is defined too broadly, those which do pose a threat may be approved. It goes without saying that sleight of hand in this area could be used by a Commission bent on an industrial policy approach to set limits to its obligation to ensure free competition. It could define the market in such a way as to permit selected mergers, while still arguing that it was fulfilling its obligation to consider primarily their effect on competition.

There are two main ways to prevent this happening. The first is to ensure that the decision-making process is subject to a maximum of transparency. The second is to shield the authority actually administering competition policy from any conflict of objective. It is with these considerations in mind that this paper has both advocated the creation of an independent European Cartel Office and considered the need to establish similar bodies for regulating the utilities and for monitoring overall support to industry. The conclusion that now is not an appropriate time to recommend such bodies in the utilities sector owes more to practical considerations than to any theoretical objection. Policy is in such a state of flux that it would be almost impossible to write a clear mandate for new institutions, let alone persuade member states to agree to their creation. Similarly, the idea of a European Industries Commission along the lines of that established in Australia is simply too revolutionary for the time being. In the short run, more practical benefits could be gained from giving DGIV a specific role in trade-policy decisions. By contrast, there is evidence of support for the idea of a European Cartel Office in the European Parliament. The policy debate has also reached the stage in which a mandate could be written quite easily, and it is possible to see how such a body could fit into the existing institutional framework.

The idea that the Commission's powers in these areas should be unbundled, with regulatory control hived off from policy formulation, is unlikely to go away. As the Commission's powers have grown in connection with the single market, so has its involvement in the actual development of policy. One argument sometimes voiced in the Commission against the idea of separate regulatory bodies is that the Commission is collectively responsible for several different policies, not just competition. Competition policy, therefore, has to be discussed and administered in connection with everything else. For example, there is no escaping the link between policy on subsidies and regional policy. Indeed, competition policy is not an end in itself, but should play a supportive role. It has to fit in and back up European policies in general.

This is tempting stuff, but it is also a recipe for confusion and disappointment. It rests on the assumption that competition policy will always be subject to compromise with one or other Community objective. As long as those compromises are struck in obscurity by a Commission that in practice has few worries about accountability, there is a risk that competition policy objectives will be overridden by other, ultimately less benign, goals. Competition, because of the benefits it brings to the consumer in terms of greater choice, and because of the efficiency it promotes in the allocation of economic resources, is a matter of public interest. Those who seek to deny this are often sectional interest groups, with their own narrow vested interests to protect. Their lobbying rarely favours more competition, and it is made easier by a secretive decision-making process. Above all there is a need for transparency of decision-making. Competition thrives in the sunshine.

There are three basic ways in which the Commission can be made accountable. The first is to member states through the Council of Ministers. In subsidy control, however, it already enjoys a great deal of autonomy. Soon it will also do so in merger regulation. In practice, the Commission is also powerful in trade policy and, if its use of Article 90 is upheld by the European Court, it will acquire formidable powers in controlling monopoly utilities. The second means is through the European Court. This is, however, less effective than it might be because the Court takes a long time to reach its decisions, because it deals with the letter of the law rather than making qualitative judgments about policy, and because its decisions (as in Philip Morris/Rothmans) can raise more questions than they answer. The third is through the European Parliament. Although it remains weak, and lacks the status and clout of national legislatures, the Parliament is likely to become more important as time goes by. It would be helped in overseeing the implementation of competition policy if that implementation were itself more transparent.

This would be one of the main practical benefits bestowed by the creation of a European Cartel Office. It should be noted that the proposal here does not envisage such an office having the final say in any merger-control decision. Its rulings could be overridden by the Commission, but public awareness that the Commission was going against the office would provoke debate, and it would have

Conclusion

to justify its actions. A similar argument could be made to apply to the concept of an Industries Commission, whose job would be to expose the costs of industrial support rather than to enforce any decisions. Independent regulatory bodies for the utilities are more difficult. Their work would be so specialized that they might need final powers of their own to function effectively.

This paper has argued that getting to grips with competition policy is a key task for the Community if the benefits of the single market are to be realized. In the end, this may well mean institutional arrangements that put competition policy on its own special footing. The challenges facing the Commission in this area are greater than ever before. They will not be easy to meet if policy towards competition continues to be regarded as just one responsibility among many in the humdrum daily life of the Commission.

Notes

1 *The Financial Times*, 24 January 1990.
2 *1992: Myths and Realities,* London Business School, 1989.
3 *The Financial Times*, 24 January 1990.

Appendix I
Selected Articles from the
EEC Treaty (1975) which are relevant
to competition

Article 3

For the purposes set out in Article 2, the activities of the Community shall include, as provided in this Treaty and in accordance with the timetable set out therein.

(a) the elimination, as between Member States, of customs duties and of quantitative restrictions on the import and export of goods, and of all other measures having equivalent effect;

(b) the establishment of a common customs tariff and of a common commercial policy towards third countries;

(c) the abolition, as between Member States, of obstacles to freedom of movement of persons, services and capital;

(d) the adoption of a common policy in the sphere of agriculture;

(e) the adoption of a common policy in the sphere of transport;

(f) the institution of a system ensuring that competition in the common market is not distorted;

(g) the application of procedures by which the economic policies of Member States can be coordinated and disequilibria in their balances of payments remedied;

(h) the approximation of the laws of Member States to the extent required for the proper functioning of the common market;

(i) the creation of a European Social Fund in order to improve employment opportunities for workers and to contribute to the raising of their standard of living;

(j) the establishment of a European Investment Bank to facilitate the economic expansion of the Community by opening up fresh resources;

(k) the association of the overseas countries and territories in order to increase trade and to promote jointly economic and social development.

Article 37

1. Member States shall progressively adjust any state monopolies of a commercial character so as to ensure that when the transitional period has ended no discrimination regarding the conditions under which goods are procured and marketed exists between nationals of Member States.

The provisions of this Article shall apply to any body through which a Member State, in law or in fact, either directly or indirectly supervises, determines or appreciably influences imports or exports between Member States. These provisions shall likewise apply to monopolies delegated by the State to others.

2. Member States shall refrain from introducing any new measure which is contrary to the principles laid down in paragraph 1 or which restricts the scope of the Articles dealing with the abolition of customs duties and quantitative restrictions between Member States.

3. The timetable for the measures referred to in paragraph 1 shall be harmonized with the abolition of quantitative restrictions on the same products provided for in Articles 30 to 34.

If the product is subject to a State monopoly of a commercial character in only one or some Member States, the Commission may authorize the other Member States to apply protective measures until the adjustment provided for in paragraph 1 has been effected; the Commission shall determine the conditions and details of such measures.

4. If a State monopoly of a commercial character has rules which are designed to make it easier to dispose of agricultural products or obtain for them the best return, steps should be taken in applying the rules contained in this Article to ensure equivalent safeguards for the employment and standard of living of the producers concerned, account being taken of the adjustments that will be possible and the specialization that will be needed with the passage of time.

5. The obligations on Member States shall be binding only in so far as they are compatible with existing international agreements.

6. With effect from the first stage the Commission shall make recommendations as to the manner in which and the timetable according to which the adjustment provided for in this Article shall be carried out.

Article 77

Aids shall be compatible with this Treaty if they meet the needs for coordination of transport or if they represent reimbursement for the discharge of certain obligations inherent in the concept of a public service.

Article 85

1. The following shall be prohibited as incompatible with the common market: all agreements between undertakings, decision by

associations of undertakings and concerted practices which may affect trade between Member States and which have as their object or effect the prevention, restriction or distortion of competition within the common market, and in particular those which:

(a) directly or indirectly fix purchase or selling prices or any other trading conditions;

(b) limit or control production, markets, technical development, or investment;

(c) share markets or sources of supply;

(d) apply dissimilar conditions to equivalent transactions with other trading parties, thereby placing them at a competitive disadvantage;

(e) make the conclusion of contracts subject to acceptance by the other parties of supplementary obligations which, by their nature or according to commercial usage, have no connection with the subject of such contracts.

2. Any agreement or decisions prohibited pursuant to this Article shall be automatically void.

3. The provisions of paragraph 1 may, however, be declared inapplicable in the case of:

– any agreement or category of agreements between undertakings;
– any decision or category of decisions by associations of undertakings;
– any concerted practice or category of concerted practices;

which contributes to improving the production or distribution of goods or to promoting technical or economic progress, while allowing consumers a fair share of the resulting benefit, and which does not

(a) impose on the undertakings concerned restrictions which are not indispensable to the attainment of these objectives;

(b) afford such undertakings the possibility of eliminating competition in respect of a substantial part of the products in question.

Article 86

Any abuse by one or more undertakings of a dominant position within the common market or in a substantial part of it shall be prohibited as incompatible with the common market in so far as it may affect trade between Member States.

Such abuse may, in particular, consist in:

(a) directly or indirectly imposing unfair purchase or selling prices or other unfair trading conditions;

(b) limiting production, markets or technical development to the prejudice of consumers;

(c) applying dissimilar conditions to equivalent transactions with other trading parties, thereby placing them at a competitive disadvantage;

(d) making the conclusion of contracts subject to acceptance by the other parties of supplementary obligations which, by their nature or according to commercial usage, have no connection with the subject of such contracts.

Article 90

1. In the case of public undertakings and undertakings to which Member States grant special or exclusive rights, Member States shall neither enact nor maintain in force any measure contrary to the rules contained in this Treaty, in particular to those rules provided for in Article 7 and Articles 85 to 94.

2. Undertakings entrusted with the operation of services of general economic interest or having the character of a revenue-producing monopoly shall be subject to rules contained in the Treaty, in particular to those rules on competition, in so far as the application of such rules does not obstruct the performance, in law or in fact, of the particular tasks assigned to them. The development of trade must not be affected to such an extent as would be contrary to the interests of the Community.

3. The Commission shall ensure the application of the provisions of this Article and shall, where necessary, address appropriate directives or decisions to Member States.

Article 92

1. Save as otherwise provided in this Treaty, any aid granted by a Member State or through State resources in any form whatsoever which distorts or threatens to distort competition by favouring certain undertakings or the production of certain goods shall, in so far as it affects trade between Member States, be incompatible with the common market.

2. The following shall be compatible with the common market:

(a) aid having a social character, granted to individual consumers, provided that such aid is granted without discrimination related to the origin of the products concerned;

(b) aid to make good the damage caused by natural disasters or exceptional circumstances;

(c) aid granted to the economy of certain areas of the Federal Republic of Germany affected by the division of Germany, in so far as such aid is required in order to compensate for the economic disadvantages caused by that division.

3. The following may be considered to be compatible with the common market:

(a) aid to promote the economic development of areas where the standard of living is abnormally low or where there is serious underemployment;

(b) aid to promote the execution of an important project of common European interest or to remedy a serious disturbance in the economy of a Member State;

(c) aid to facilitate the development of certain economic activities or of certain economic areas, where such aid does not adversely affect trading conditions to an extent contrary to the common interest. However, the aids granted to shipbuilding as of 1 January 1957 shall, in so far as they serve only to compensate for the absence of customs protection, be progressively reduced under the same conditions as apply to the elimination of customs duties, subject to the provisions of this Treaty concerning common commercial policy towards third countries;

(d) such other categories of aid as may be specified by decision of the Council acting by a qualified majority on a proposal from the Commission.

Article 93

1. The Commission shall, in cooperation with Member States, keep under constant review all systems of aid existing in those States. It shall propose to the latter any appropriate measures required by the progressive development or by the functioning of the common market.

2. If, after giving notice to the parties concerned to submit their comments, the Commission finds that aid granted by a State or through State resources is not compatible with the common market having regard to Article 92, or that such aid is being misused, it shall decide that the State concerned shall abolish or alter such aid within a period of time to be determined by the Commission.

If the State concerned does not comply with this decision within the prescribed time, the Commission or any other interested State may, in derogation from the provisions of Articles 169 and 170, refer the matter to the Court of Justice direct.

On application by a Member State, the Council may, acting unanimously, decide that aid which that State is granting or intends to grant shall be considered to be compatible with the common market, in derogation from the provisions of Article 92 or from the regulations provided for in Article 94, if such a decision is justified by exceptional circumstances. If, as regards the aid in question, the Commission has already initiated the procedure provided for in the first subparagraph of this paragraph, the fact that the State concerned has made its application to the Council shall have the effect of suspending that procedure until the Council has made its attitude known.

If, however, the Council has not made its attitude known within three months of the said application being made, the Commission shall give its decision on the case.

3. The Commission shall be informed, in sufficient time to enable it to submit its comments, of any plans to grant or alter aid. If it considers that any such plan is not compatible with the common market having regard to Article 92, it shall without delay initiate the procedure provided for in paragraph 2. The Member State concerned shall not put its proposed measure into effect until this procedure has resulted in a final decision.

Article 100a

1. By way of derogation from Article 100 and save where otherwise provided in this Treaty, the following provisions shall apply for the achievement of the objectives set out in Article 8a. The Council shall, acting by a qualified majority on a proposal from the Commission in cooperation with the European Parliament and after consulting the Economic and Social Committee, adopt the measures for the approximation of the provisions laid down by law, regulation or administrative action in Member States which have as their object the establishment and functioning of the internal market.

2. Paragraph 1 shall not apply to fiscal provisions, to those relating to the free movement of persons nor to those relating to the rights and interests of employed persons.

3. The Commission, in its proposals envisaged in paragraph 1 concerning health, safety, environmental protection and consumer protection, will take as a base a high level of protection.

4. If, after the adoption of a harmonization measure by the Council acting by a qualified majority, a Member State deems it necessary to apply national provisions on grounds of major needs referred to in Article 36, or relating to protection of the environment or the working environment, it shall notify the Commission of these provisions.

The Commission shall confirm the provisions involved after having verified that they are not a means of arbitrary discrimination or a disguised restriction on trade between Member States.

By way of derogation from the procedure laid down in Articles 169 and 170, the Commission or any Member State may bring the matter directly before the Court of Justice if it considers that another Member State is making improper use of the powers provided for in this Article.

5. The harmonization measures referred to above shall, in appropriate cases, include a safeguard clause authorizing the Member

States to take, for one or more of the non-economic reasons referred to in Article 36, provisional measures subject to a Community control procedure.

Article 222
This Treaty shall in no way prejudice the rules in Member States governing the system of property ownership.

Appendix II
Text of Merger Control Regulation (EEC) No. 4064/89 of 21 December 1989

THE COUNCIL OF THE EUROPEAN COMMUNITIES

Having regard to the Treaty establishing the European Economic Community, and in particular Articles 87 and 235 thereof,

Having regard to the proposal from the Commission,

Having regard to the opinion of the European Parliament,

Having regard to the opinion of the Economic and Social Committee,

Whereas, for the achievement of the aims of the Treaty establishing the European Economic Community, Article 3(f) gives the Community the objective of instituting 'a system ensuring that competition in the common market is not distorted';

Whereas this system is essential for the achievement of the internal market by 1992 and its further development;

Whereas the dismantling of internal frontiers is resulting and will continue to result in major corporate re-organizations in the Community, particularly in the form of concentrations;

Whereas such a development must be welcomed as being in line with the requirements of dynamic competition and capable of increasing the competitiveness of European industry, improving the conditions of growth and raising the standard of living in the Community;

Whereas, however, it must be ensured that the process of re-organization does not result in lasting damage to competition; whereas the Community law must therefore include provisions governing those concentrations which may significantly impede effective competition in the common market or in a substantial part of it;

Whereas Articles 85 and 86, while applicable, according to the case-law of the Court of Justice, to certain concentrations, are not, however, sufficient to cover all operations which may prove to be incompatible with the system of undistorted competition envisaged in the Treaty;

Whereas a new legal instrument should therefore be created in the form of a Regulation to permit effective monitoring of all concentrations from the point of view of their effect on the structure of competition in the Community and to be the only instrument applicable to such concentrations;

Whereas this Regulation should therefore be based not only on Article 87 but, principally, on Article 235 of the Treaty, under which the Community may give itself the additional powers of action necessary for the attainment of its objectives, and also with regard to concentrations on the markets for agricultural products listed in Annex II to the Treaty;

Whereas the provisions to be adopted in this Regulation should apply to significant structural changes the impact of which on the market goes beyond the national borders of any one Member State;

Whereas the scope of application of this regulation should therefore be defined according to the geographical area of activity of the undertakings concerned and be limited by quantitative thresholds in order to cover those concentrations which have a Community dimension; whereas, at the end of an initial phase of the implementation of this Regulation, these thresholds should be reviewed in the light of the experience gained;

Whereas a concentration with a Community dimension exists where the aggregate turnover of the undertakings concerned exceeds given levels worldwide and throughout the Community and where at least two of the undertakings concerned have their sole or main fields of activities in different Member States or where, although the undertakings in question act mainly in one and the same Member State, at least one of them has substantial operations in at least one other Member State; whereas that is also the case where the concentrations are effected by undertakings which do not have their principal fields of activities in the Community but which have substantial operations there;

Whereas the arrangements to be introduced for the control of concentrations should, without prejudice to Article 90(2) of the Treaty, respect the principle of non-discrimination between the public and the private sectors; whereas, in the public sector, calculation of the turnover of an undertaking concerned in a concentration needs, therefore, to take account of undertakings making up an economic unit with an independent power of decision, irrespective of the way in which their capital is held or of the rules of administrative supervision applicable to them;

Whereas it is necessary to establish whether concentrations with a Community dimension are compatible or not with the common market from the point of view of the need to preserve and develop effective competition in the common market; whereas, in so doing, the

113

Commission must place its appraisal within the general framework of the achievement of the fundamental objectives referred to in Article 2 of the Treaty, including that of strengthening the Community's economic and social cohesion, referred to in Article 130a;

Whereas this Regulation should establish the principle that a concentration with a Community dimension which creates or strengthens a position as a result of which effective competition in the common market or in a substantial part of it is significantly impeded is to be declared incompatible with the common market;

Whereas concentrations which, by reason of the limited market share of the undertakings concerned, are not liable to impede effective competition may be presumed to be compatible with the common market; whereas, without prejudice to Articles 85 and 86 of the Treaty, an indication to this effect exists, in particular, where the market share of the undertakings concerned does not exceed 25% either in the common market or in a substantial part of it;

Whereas the Commission should have the task of taking all the decisions necessary to establish whether or not concentrations of a Community dimension are compatible with the common market, as well as decisions designed to restore effective competition;

Whereas to ensure effective control undertakings should be obliged to give prior notification of concentrations with a Community dimension and provision should be made for the suspension of concentrations for a limited period, and for the possibility of extending or waiving a suspension where necessary; whereas in the interests of legal certainty the validity of transactions must nevertheless be protected as much as necessary;

Whereas a period within which the Commission must initiate a proceeding in respect of a notified concentration and a period within which it must give a final decision on the compatibility or incompatibility with the common market of a notified concentration should be laid down;

Whereas the undertakings concerned must be accorded the right to be heard by the Commission as soon as a proceeding has been initiated; whereas the members of management and supervisory organs and recognized workers' representatives in the undertakings concerned, together with third parties showing a legitimate interest, must also be given the opportunity to be heard;

Whereas the Commission should act in close and constant liaison with the competent authorities of the Member States from which it obtains comments and information;

Whereas, for the purposes of this Regulation, and in accordance with the case-law of the Court of Justice, the Commission must be afforded the assistance of Member States and must also be empowered to require information to be given and to carry out the necessary investigations in order to appraise concentrations;

Whereas compliance with this Regulation must be enforceable by means of fines and periodic penalty payments; whereas the Court of Justice should be given unlimited jurisdiction in that regard pursuant to Article 172 of the Treaty;

Whereas it is appropriate to define the concept of concentration in such a manner as to cover only operations bringing about a durable change in the structure of the undertakings concerned; whereas it is therefore necessary to exclude from the scope of this Regulation those operations which have as their object or effect the coordination of the competitive behaviour of independent undertakings, since such operations fall to be examined under the appropriate provisions of Regulations implementing Article 85 or Article 86 of the Treaty; whereas it is appropriate to make this distinction specifically in the case of the creation of joint ventures;

Whereas there is no coordination of competitive behaviour within the meaning of this Regulation where two or more undertakings agree to acquire jointly control of one or more other undertakings with the object and effect of sharing amongst themselves such undertakings or their assets;

Whereas the application of this Regulation is not excluded where the undertakings concerned accept restrictions directly related and necessary to the implementation of the concentration;

Whereas the Commission should be given exclusive competence to apply this Regulation, subject to review by the Court of Justice;

Whereas the Member States may not apply their national legislation on competition to concentrations with a Community dimension, unless the Regulation makes provision therefor; whereas the relevant powers of national authorities should be limited to cases where, failing intervention by the Commission, effective competition is likely to be significantly impeded within the territory of a Member State and where the competition interests of that Member State cannot be sufficiently protected otherwise than by this Regulation; whereas the Member States concerned must act promptly in such cases; whereas this Regulation cannot, because of the diversity of national law, fix a single deadline for the adoption of remedies;

Whereas, furthermore, the exclusive application of this Regulation to concentrations with a Community dimension is without prejudice to Article 223 of the Treaty, and does not prevent the Member States' taking appropriate measures to protect legitimate interests other than those pursued by this Regulation, provided that such measures are compatible with the general principles and other provisions of Community law;

Whereas concentrations not referred to in this Regulation come, in principle, within the jurisdiction of the Member States; whereas, however, the Commission should have the power to act, at the request of a Member State concerned, in cases where effective competition would be significantly impeded within that Member State's territory;

Whereas the conditions in which concentrations involving Community undertakings are carried out in non-member countries should be observed, and provision should be made for the possibility of the Council's giving the Commission an appropriate mandate for negotiations with a view to obtaining non-discriminatory treatment for Community undertakings;

Whereas this Regulation in no way detracts from the collective rights of workers as recognized in the undertakings concerned,

HAS ADOPTED THIS REGULATION:

Article 1

Scope

1. Without prejudice to Article 22 this Regulation shall apply to all concentrations with a Community dimension as defined in paragraph 2.

2. For the purposes of this Regulation, a concentration with a Community dimension where;

(a) the aggregate worldwide turnover of all the undertakings concerned is more than ECU 5,000 million, and

(b) the aggregate Community-wide turnover of each of at least two of the undertakings concerned is more than ECU 250 million,

unless each of the undertakings concerned achieves more than two-thirds of its aggregate Community-wide turnover within one and the same Member State.

3. The thresholds laid down in paragraph 2 will be reviewed before the end of the fourth year following that of the adoption of this regulation by the Council acting by a qualified majority on a proposal from the Commission.

Article 2

Appraisal of concentrations

1. Concentrations within the scope of this Regulation shall be appraised in accordance with the following provisions with a view to establishing whether or not they are compatible with the common market.

In making this appraisal, the Commission shall take into account:

(a) the need to preserve and develop effective competition within the common market in view of, among other things, the structure of all the markets concerned and the actual or potential competition from undertakings located either within or without the Community;

(b) the market position of the undertakings concerned and their economic and financial power, the opportunities available to suppliers and users, their access to supplies or markets, any legal or other barriers to entry, supply and demand trends for the relevant goods and services, the interests of the immediate and ultimate consumers, and the development of technical and economic progress provided that it is to consumers' advantage and does not form an obstacle to competition.

2. A concentration which does not create or strengthen a dominant position as a result of which effective competition would be significantly impeded in the common market or in a substantial part of it shall be declared compatible with the common market.

3. A concentration which creates or strengthens a dominant position as a result of which competition would be significantly impeded in the common market or in a substantial part of it shall be declared incompatible with the common market.

Article 3

Definition of concentration

1. A concentration shall be deemed to arise where:

(a) two or more previously independent undertakings merge, or

(b) one or more persons already controlling at least one undertaking, or

– one or more undertakings

acquire, whether by purchase of securities or assets, by contract or by other means, direct or indirect control of the whole or parts of one or more other undertakings.

2. An operation, including the creation of a joint venture, which has as its object or effect the coordination of the competitive behaviour of undertakings which remain independent shall not constitute a concentration within the meaning of paragraph 1(b).

The creation of a joint venture performing on a lasting basis all the functions of an autonomous economic entity, which does not give rise to coordination of the competitive behaviour of the parties amongst themselves or between them and the joint venture, shall constitute a concentration within the meaning of paragraph 1(b).

3. For the purposes of this Regulation, control shall be constituted by rights, contracts or any other means which, either separately or jointly and having regard to the considerations of fact or law involved, confer the possibility of exercising decisive influence on an undertaking, in particular by:

(a) ownership or the right to use all or part of the assets of an undertaking;

(b) rights or contracts which confer decisive influence on the composition, voting or decisions of the organs of an undertaking.

4. Control is acquired by persons or undertakings which:

(a) are holders of the rights or entitled to rights under the contracts concerned, or

(b) while not being holders of such rights or entitled to rights under such contracts, have the power to exercise the rights deriving therefrom.

5. A concentration shall not be deemed to arise where:

(a) credit institutions or other financial institutions or insurance companies, the normal activities of which include transactions and dealing in securities for their own account or for the account of others, hold on a temporary basis securities which they have acquired in an undertaking with a view to reselling them, provided that they do not exercise voting rights in respect of those securities with a view to determining the competitive behaviour of that undertaking or provided that they exercise such voting rights only with a view to preparing the sale of all or part of that under taking or of its assets or the sale of those securities and that any such sale takes place within one year of the date of acquisition; that period may be extended by the Commission on request where such institutions or companies justify the fact that the sale was not reasonably possible within the period set;

(b) control is acquired by an office holder according to the laws of a Member State relating to liquidation, winding up, insolvency, cessation of payments, compositions or analogous proceedings;

(c) the operations referred to in paragraph 1(b) are carried out by the financial holding companies referred to in Article 5(3) of the Fourth Council Directive 78/660/EEC of 25 July 1978 on the annual accounts of certain types of companies, as last amended by Directive 84/569/EEC, provided however that the voting rights in respect of the holding are exercised, in particular in relation to the appointment of members of the management and supervisory bodies of the undertakings in which they have holdings, only to maintain the full value of those investments and not to determine directly or indirectly the competitive conduct of those undertakings.

Article 4

Prior notification of concentrations

1. Concentrations with a Community dimension as referred to by this Regulation shall be notified to the Commission not more than one week after the conclusion of the agreement, or the announcement of the public bid, or the acquisition of a controlling interest. That week shall begin when the first of those events occurs.

2. A concentration which consists of a merger within the meaning of Article 3(1)(a) or in the acquisition of joint control within the meaning of Article 3(1)(b) shall be notified jointly by the parties to the merger or by those acquiring joint control as the case may be. In all other cases, the notification shall be effected by the person or undertaking acquiring control of the whole or parts of one or more undertakings.

3. Where the Commission finds that a notified concentration falls within the scope of this Regulation, it shall publish the fact of the notification, at the same time indicating the names of the parties, the nature of the concentration and the economic sectors involved. The Commission shall take account of the legitimate interest of undertakings in the protection of their business secrets.

Article 5

Calculation of turnover

1. Aggregate turnover within the meaning of Article 1(2) shall comprise the amounts derived by the undertakings concerned in the preceding financial year from the sale of the products and the provision of services falling within the undertakings' ordinary activities after the deduction of sales rebates and of value added tax and other taxes directly related to turnover. The aggregate turnover of an undertaking concerned shall not include the sale of products or the provision of services between any of the undertakings referred in paragraph 4.

Turnover, in the Community or in a Member State, shall comprise products sold and services provided to undertakings or consumers, in the Community or in that Member State as the case may be.

2. By way of derogation from paragraph 1, where the concentration consists in the acquisition of parts, whether or not constituted as legal entities, of one or more undertakings, only the turnover relating to the parts which are the subject of the transaction shall be taken into account with regard to the seller or sellers.

However, two or more transactions within the meaning of the first subparagraph which take place within a two-year period between the same persons or undertakings shall be treated as one and the same concentration arising on the date of the last transaction.

3. In place of turnover the following shall be used:

(a) for credit institutions and other financial institutions, as regards Article 1(2)(a), one-tenth of their total assets.

As regards Article 1(2)(b) and the final part of Article 1(2), total Community-wide turnover shall be replaced by one-tenth of total assets multiplied by the ratio between loans and advances to credit institutions and customers in transactions with Community residents and the total sum of those loans and advances.

As regards the final part of Article 1(2), total turnover within one Member State shall be replaced by one-tenth of total assets multiplied by the ratio between loans and advances to credit institutions and customers in transactions with residents of that Member State and the total sum of those loans and advances;

(b) for insurance undertakings, the value of gross premiums written which shall comprise all amounts received and receivable in respect of insurance contracts issued by or on behalf of the insurance undertakings, including also outgoing reinsurance premiums, and after deduction of taxes and parafiscal contributions or levies charged by reference to the amounts of individual premiums or the total volume of premiums; as regards Article 1(2)(b) and the final part of Article 1(2), gross premiums received from the Community residents and from residents of one Member State respectively shall be taken into account.

4. Without prejudice to paragraph 2, the turnover of an undertaking concerned within the meaning of Article 1(2) shall be calculated by adding together the respective turnover of the following:

(a) the undertaking concerned;
(b) those undertakings in which the undertaking concerned, directly or indirectly;

- owns more than half the capital or business assets, or
- has the power to exercise more than half the voting rights, or
- has the power to appoint more than half the members of the supervisory board, the administrative board or bodies legally representing the undertakings, or
- has the right to manage the undertakings' affairs;

(c) those undertakings which have in an undertaking concerned the rights or powers listed in (b);

(d) those undertakings in which an undertaking as referred to in (c) has the right or powers listed in (b);

(e) those undertakings in which two or more undertakings as referred to in (a) to (d) jointly have the rights or powers listed in (b).

5. Where undertakings concerned by the concentration jointly have the rights or powers listed in paragraph 4(b), in calculating the turnover of the undertakings concerned for the purposes of Article 1(2);

(a) no account shall be taken of the turnover resulting from the sale of products or the provision of services between the joint undertaking and each of the undertakings concerned or any other undertaking connected with any one of them, as set out in paragraph 4(b) to (e);

(b) account shall be taken of the turnover resulting from the sale of products and the provision of services between the joint undertaking and any third undertakings. This turnover shall be apportioned equally amongst the undertakings concerned.

Article 6

Examination of the notification and initiation of proceedings

1. The Commission shall examine the notification as soon as it is received.

(a) Where it concludes that the concentration notified does not fall within the scope of this Regulation, it shall record that finding by means of a decision.

(b) Where it finds that the concentration notified, although falling within the scope of this Regulation, does not raise serious doubts as to its compatibility with the common market, it shall decide not to oppose it and shall declare that it is compatible with the common market.

(c) If, on the other hand, it finds that the concentration notified falls within the scope of this Regulation and raises serious doubts as to its compatibility with the common market, it shall decide to initiate proceedings.

2. The Commission shall notify its decision to the undertakings concerned and the competent authorities of the Member States without delay.

Article 7

Suspension of concentrations

1. For the purposes of paragraph 2 a concentration as defined in Article 1 shall not be put into effect either before its notification or within the first three weeks following its notification.

2. Where the Commission, following a preliminary examination of the notification within the period provided for in paragraph 1, finds it necessary in order to ensure the full effectiveness of any decision taken later pursuant to Article 8(3) and (4), it may decide on its own initiative to continue the suspension of a concentration in whole or in part until it takes a final decision, or to take other interim measures to that effect.

3. Paragraphs 1 and 2 shall not impede the implementation of a public bid which has been notified to the Commission in accordance with Article 4(1) by the date of its announcement, provided that the acquirer does not exercise the voting rights attached to the securities in question or does so only to maintain the full value of those investments and on the basis of a derogation granted by the Commission pursuant to paragraph 4.

4. The Commission may, on request, grant a derogation from the obligations imposed in paragraphs 1, 2 or 3 in order to prevent serious damage to one or more undertakings concerned by a concentration or to a third party. That derogation may be made subject to conditions and obligations in order to ensure conditions of effective competition. A derogation may be applied for and granted at any time, even before notification or after the transaction.

5. The validity of any transaction carried out in contravention of paragraph 1 or 2 shall be dependent on a decision pursuant to Article 6(1)(b) or 8(2) or (3) or by virtue of the presumption established by Article 10(6).

This Article shall, however, have no effect on the validity of transactions in securities including those convertible into other securities admitted to trading on a market which is regulated and supervised by authorities recognized by public bodies, operates regularly and is accessible directly or indirectly to the public, unless the buyer and seller knew or ought to have known that the transaction was carried out in contravention of paragraph 1 or 2.

Article 8

Powers of decision of the Commission

1. Without prejudice to Article 9, each proceeding initiated pursuant to Article 6(1)(c) shall be closed by means of a decision provided for in paragraphs 2 to 5.

2. Where the Commission finds that following modifications by the undertakings concerned if necessary, a notified concentration fulfils the criterion laid down in Article 2(2), it shall issue a decision declaring the concentration compatible within the common market.

It may attach to its decision conditions and obligations intended to ensure that the undertakings concerned comply with the commitments they have entered into *vis-à-vis* the Commission with a view to modifying the original concentration plan. The decision declaring the concentration compatible shall also cover restrictions directly related and necessary to the implementation of the concentration.

3. Where the Commission finds that a concentration fulfils the criterion laid down in Article 2(3), it shall issue a decision declaring that the concentration is incompatible with the common market.

4. Where a concentration has already been implemented, the Commission may, in a decision pursuant to paragraph 3 or by a separate decision, require the undertakings or assets brought together to be separated or the cessation of joint control or any other action that may be appropriate in order to restore conditions of effective competition.

5. The Commission may revoke the decision it has taken pursuant to paragraph 2 where:

(a) the declaration of compatibility is based on incorrect information for which one of the undertakings concerned is responsible or where it has been obtained by deceit, or

(b) the undertakings concerned commit a breach of an obligation attached to the decision.

6. In the case referred to in paragraph 5, the Commission may take a decision pursuant to paragraph 3, without being bound by the deadline referred to in Article 10(3).

Article 9

Referral to the competent authorities of the Member States

1. The Commission may, by means of a decision notified without delay to the undertakings concerned and the competent authorities of the other Member States, refer a notified concentration to the competent authorities of the Member State concerned in the following circumstances.

2. Within three weeks of the date of receipt of the copy of the notification a Member State may inform the Commission which shall inform the undertakings concerned that a concentration threatens to create or to strengthen a dominant position as a result of which effective

competition would be significantly impeded on a market, within that Member State, which presents all the characteristics of a distinct market, be it a substantial part of the common market or not.

3. If the Commission considers that, having regard to the market for the products or services in question and the geographical reference market within the meaning of paragraph 7, there is such a distinct market and that such a threat exists either:

(a) it shall itself deal with the case in order to maintain or restore effective competition on the market concerned, or

(b) it shall refer the case to the competent authorities of the Member State concerned with a view to the application of that State's national competition law.

If, however, the Commission considers that such a distinct market or threat does not exist it shall adopt a decision to that effect which it shall address to the Member State concerned.

4. A decision to refer or not to refer pursuant to paragraph 3 shall be taken where:

(a) as a general rule within the six-week period provided for in Article 10(1), second subparagraph, where the Commission has not initiated proceedings pursuant to Article 6(1)(b), or

(b) within three months at most of the notification of the concentration concerned where the Commission has initiated proceedings under Article 6(1)(c), without taking the preparatory steps in order to adopt the necessary measures pursuant to Article 8(2), second subparagraph, (3) or (4) to maintain or restore effective competition on the market concerned.

5. If within the three months referred to in paragraph 4(b) the Commission, despite a reminder from the Member State concerned, has taken no decision on referral in accordance with paragraph 3 or taken the preparatory steps referred to in paragraph 4(b), it shall be deemed to have taken a decision to refer the case to the Member State concerned in accordance with paragraph 3(b).

6. The publication of any report or the announcement of the findings of the examination of the concentration by the competent authority of the Member State concerned shall be effected not more than four months after the Commission's referral.

7. The geographical reference market shall consist of the area in which the undertakings concerned are involved in the supply of products or services, in which the conditions of competition are sufficiently homogeneous and which can be distinguished from neighbouring areas

because, in particular, conditions of competition are appreciably different in those areas. This assessment should take account in particular of the nature and characteristics of the products or services concerned, of the existence of entry barriers or of consumer preferences, of appreciable differences of the undertakings' market shares between neighbouring areas or of substantial price differences.

8. In applying the provisions of this Article, the Member State concerned may take only the measure strictly necessary to safeguard or restore effective competition on the market concerned.

9. In accordance with the relevant provisions of the Treaty, any Member State may appeal to the Court of Justice, and in particular request the application of Article 186, for the purpose of applying its national competition law.

10. This Article will be reviewed before the end of the fourth year following that of the adoption of this Regulation.

Article 10

Time limits for initiating proceedings and for decisions

1. The decisions referred to in Article 6(1) must be taken within one month at most. The period shall begin on the day following the receipt of a notification or, if the information to be supplied with the notification is incomplete, on the day following the receipt of the complete information.

That period shall be increased to six weeks if the Commission receives a request from a Member State in accordance with Article 9(2).

2. Decisions taken pursuant to Article 8(2) concerning notified concentrations must be taken as soon as it appears that the serious doubts referred to in Article 6(1)(c) have been removed, particularly as a result of modifications made by the undertakings concerned, and at the latest by the deadline laid down in paragraph 3.

3. Without prejudice to Article 8(6), decisions taken pursuant to Article 8(3) concerning notified concentrations must be taken within not more than four months of the date on which the proceeding is initiated.

4. The period set by paragraph 3 shall exceptionally be suspended where, owing to circumstances for which one of the undertakings involved in the concentration is responsible, the Commission has had to request information by decision pursuant to Article 11 or to order an investigation pursuant to Article 13.

5. Where the Court of Justice gives a judgment which annuls the whole or part of a Commission decision taken under this Regulation, the periods laid down in this Regulation shall start again from the date of the judgment.

6. Where the Commission has not taken a decision in accordance with Article 6(1)(b) or (c) or Article 8(2) or (3) within the deadlines set in paragraphs 1 and 3 respectively, the concentration shall be deemed declared compatible with the common market, without prejudice to Article 9.

Article 11

Request for information

1. In carrying out the duties assigned to it by this Regulation, the Commission may obtain all necessary information from the Governments and competent authorities of the Member States, from the persons referred to in Article 3(1)(b), and from undertakings and associations of undertakings.

2. When sending a request for information to a person, an undertaking or an association of undertakings, the Commission shall at the same time send a copy of the request to the competent authority of the Member State within the territory of which the residence of the person or the seat of the undertaking or association of undertakings is situated.

3. In its request the Commission shall state the legal basis and the purpose of the request and also the penalties provided for in Article 14(1)(b) for supplying incorrect information.

4. The information requested shall be provided, in the case of undertakings, by their owners or their representatives and, in the case of legal persons, companies or firms, or of associations having no legal personality, by the persons authorized to represent them by law or by their statutes.

5. Where a person, an undertaking or an association of undertakings does not provide the information requested within the period fixed by the Commission or provides incomplete information, the Commission shall by decision require the information to be provided. The decision shall specify what information is required, fix an appropriate period within which it is to be supplied and state the penalties provided for in Articles 14(1)(b) and 15(1)(a) and the right to have the decision reviewed by the Court of Justice.

6. The Commission shall at the same time send a copy of its decision to the competent authority of the Member State within the territory of which the residence of the person or the seat of the undertaking or association of undertakings is situated.

Article 12

Investigations by the authorities of the Member States

1. At the request of the Commission, the competent authorities of the Member States shall undertake the investigations which the Commission considers to be necessary pursuant to Article 13(1), or which it has ordered by decision pursuant to Article 13(3). The officials of the competent authorities of the Member States responsible for conducting those investigations shall exercise their powers upon production of an authorization in writing issued by the competent authority of the Member State within the territory of which the investigation is to be carried out. Such authorization shall specify the subject matter and purpose of the investigation.

2. If so requested by the Commission or by the competent authority of the Member State within the territory of which the investigation is to be carried out, officials of the Commission may assist the officials of that authority in carrying out their duties.

Article 13

Investigative powers of the Commission

1. In carrying out the duties assigned to it by this Regulation, the Commission may undertake all necessary investigations into undertakings and associations of undertakings.

To that end the officials authorized by the Commission shall be empowered:

(a) to examine the books and other business records;

(b) to take or demand copies of extracts from the books and business records;

(c) to ask for oral explanations on the spot;

(d) to enter any premises, land and means of transport of undertakings.

2. The officials of the Commission authorized to carry out the investigations shall exercise their powers on production of an authorization in writing specifying the subject matter and purpose of the investigation and the penalties provided for in Article 14(1)(c) in cases where production of the required books or other business records is incomplete. In good time before the investigation, the Commission shall inform, in writing, the competent authority of the Member State within the territory of which the investigation is to be carried out of the investigation and of the identities of the authorized officials.

3. Undertakings and associations of undertakings shall submit to investigations ordered by decision of the Commission. The decision shall specify the subject matter and purpose of the investigation, appoint the date on which it shall begin and state the penalties provided for in Articles 14(1)(c) and 15(1)(b) and the right to have the decision reviewed by the Court of Justice.

4. The Commission shall in good time and in writing inform the competent authority of the Member State within the territory of which the investigation is to be carried out of its intention of taking a decision pursuant to paragraph 3. It shall hear the competent authority before taking its decision.

5. Officials of the competent authority of the Member State within the territory of which the investigation is to be carried out may, at the request of that authority or of the Commission, assist the officials of the Commission in carrying out their duties.

6. Where an undertaking or association of undertakings opposes an investigation ordered pursuant to this Article, the Member State concerned shall afford the necessary assistance to the officials authorized by the Commission to enable them to carry out their investigation. To this end the Member State shall, after consulting the Commission, take the necessary measures within one year of the entry into force of this Regulation.

Article 14

Fines

1. The Commission may by decision impose on the persons referred to in Article 3(1)(b), undertakings or associations of undertakings fines of from Ecu 1,000 to 50,000 where intentionally or negligently:

(a) they omit to notify a concentration in accordance with Article 4;

(b) they supply incorrect or misleading information in a notification pursuant to Article 4;

(c) they supply incorrect information in response to a request made pursuant to Article 11 or fail to supply information within the period fixed by a decision taken pursuant to Article 11;

(d) they produce the required books or other business records in incomplete form during investigations pursuant to Articles 12 or 13, or refuse to submit to an investigation ordered by decision taken pursuant to Article 13.

2. The Commission may by decision impose fines not exceeding 10% of the aggregate turnover of the undertakings concerned within the

meaning of Article 5 on the persons or undertakings concerned where, either intentionally or negligently, they;

(a) fail to comply with an obligation imposed by decision pursuant to Article 7(4) or 8(2), second subparagraph;

(b) put into effect a concentration in breach of Article 7(1) or disregard a decision taken pursuant to Article 7(2);

(c) put into effect a concentration declared incompatible with the common market by decision pursuant to Article 8(3) or do not take the measures ordered by decision pursuant to Article 8(4).

3. In setting the amount of a fine, regard shall be had to the nature and gravity of the infringement.

4. Decisions taken pursuant to paragraphs 1 and 2 shall not be of a criminal law nature.

Article 15

Periodic penalty payments

1. The Commission may by decision impose on the persons referred to in Article 3(1)(b), undertakings or associations of undertakings concerned periodic penalty payments of up to Ecu 25,000 for each day of the delay calculated from the date set in the decision, in order to compel them:

(a) to supply complete and correct information which it has requested by decision pursuant to Article 11;

(b) to submit to an investigation which it has ordered by decision pursuant to Article 13.

2. The Commission may by decision impose on the persons referred to in Article 3(1)(b) or on undertakings periodic penalty payments of up to ECU 100,000 for each day of the delay calculated from the date set in the decision, in order to compel them:

(a) to comply with an obligation imposed by decision pursuant to Article 7(4) or 8(2), second subparagraph, or

(b) to apply the measures ordered by decision pursuant to Article 8(4).

3. Where the persons referred to in Article 3(1)(b), undertakings or associations of undertakings have satisfied the obligation which it was the

purpose of the periodic penalty payment to enforce, the Commission may set the total amount of the periodic penalty payments at a lower figure than that which would arise under the original decision.

Article 16

Review by the Court of Justice

The Court of Justice shall have unlimited jurisdiction within the meaning of Article 172 of the Treaty to review decisions whereby the Commission has fixed a fine or periodic penalty payments; it may cancel, reduce or increase the fine or periodic penalty payment imposed.

Article 17

Professional secrecy

1. Information acquired as a result of the application of Articles 11, 12, 13 and 18 shall be used only for the purposes of the relevant request, investigation or hearing.

2. Without prejudice to Articles 4(3), 18 and 20, the Commission and competent authorities of the Member States, their officials and other servants shall not disclose information they have acquired through the application of this Regulation of the kind covered by the obligation of professional secrecy.

3. Paragraphs 1 and 2 shall not prevent publication of general information or of surveys which do not contain information relating to particular undertakings or associations of undertakings.

Article 18

Hearing of the parties and of third persons

1. Before taking any decision provided for in Article 7(2) and (4), 8(2), second subparagraph, and (3) to (5), 14 and 15, the Commission shall give the persons, undertakings and associations of undertakings concerned the opportunity, at every stage of the procedure up to the consultation of the Advisory Committee, of making known their views on the objections against them.

2. By way of derogation from paragraph 1, a decision to continue the suspension of a concentration or to grant a derogation from suspension as referred to in Article 7(2) or (4) may be taken provisionally, without the persons, undertakings and associations of undertakings concerned being

given the opportunity to make known their views beforehand, provided that the Commission gives them that opportunity as soon as possible after having taken its decision.

3. The Commission shall base its decision only on objections on which the parties have been able to submit their observations. The rights of the defence shall be fully respected in the proceedings. Access to the file shall be open at least to the parties directly involved, subject to the legitimate interest of undertakings in the protection of the business secrets.

4. Insofar as the Commission and the competent authorities of the Member States deem it necessary, they may also hear other natural or legal persons. Natural or legal persons showing a legitimate interest and especially members of the administrative or management organs of the undertakings concerned or recognized workers' representatives of those undertakings shall be entitled, upon application, to be heard.

Article 19

Liaison with the authorities of the Member States

1. The Commission shall transmit to the competent authorities of the Member States copies of notifications within three working days and, as soon as possible, copies of the most important documents lodged with or issued by the Commission pursuant to this Regulation.

2. The Commission shall carry out the procedures set out in this regulation in close and constant liaison with the competent authorities of the Member States, which may express their views upon those procedures. For the purposes of Article 9 it shall obtain information from the competent authority of the Member State as referred to in paragraph 2 of that Article and give it the opportunity to make known its views at every stage of the procedure up to the adoption of a decision pursuant to paragraph 3 of that Article; to that end it shall give it access to the file.

3. An Advisory Committee on concentrations shall be consulted before any decision is taken pursuant to Articles 8(2) to (5), 14 or 15, or any provisions are adopted pursuant to Article 23.

4. The Advisory Committee shall consist of representatives of the authorities of the Member States. Each Member State shall appoint one or two representatives; if unable to attend, they may be replaced by other representatives. At least one of the representatives of a Member State shall be competent in matters of restrictive practices and dominant positions.

5. Consultation shall take place at a joint meeting convened at the invitation of and chaired by the Commission. A summary of the facts,

together with the most important documents and a preliminary draft of the decision to be taken for each case considered, shall be sent with the invitation. The meeting shall take place not less than 14 days after the invitation has been sent. The Commission may in exceptional cases shorten that period as appropriate in order to avoid serious harm to one or more of the undertakings concerned by a concentration.

6. The Advisory Committee shall deliver an opinion on the Commission's draft decision, if necessary by taking a vote. The Advisory Committee may deliver an opinion even if some members are absent and unrepresented. The opinion shall be delivered in writing and appended to the draft decision. The Commission shall take the utmost account of the opinion delivered by the Committee. It shall inform the Committee of the manner in which its opinion has been taken into account.

7. The Advisory Committee may recommend publication of the opinion. The Commission may carry out such publication. The decision to publish shall take due account of the legitimate interest of undertakings in the protection of their business secrets and of the interest of the undertakings concerned in such publication taking place.

Article 20

Publication of decisions

1. The Commission shall publish the decisions which it takes pursuant to Article 8(2), where conditions and obligations are attached to them, and to Article 8(2) to (5) in the Official Journal of the European Communities.

2. The publication shall state the names of the parties and the main content of the decision; it shall have regard to the legitimate interest of undertakings in the protection of their business secrets.

Article 21

Jurisdiction

1. Subject to review by the Court of Justice, the Commission shall have sole competence to take the decisions provided for in this Regulation.

2. No Member State shall apply its national legislation on competition to any concentration that has a Community dimension.

The first subparagraph shall be without prejudice to any Member State's power to carry out any enquiries necessary for the application of Article 9(2) or after referral, pursuant Article 9(3), first subparagraph, indent (b), or (5), to take the measures strictly necessary for the application of Article 9(8).

3. Notwithstanding paragraphs 1 and 2, Member States may take appropriate measures to protect legitimate interests other than those taken into consideration by this Regulation and compatible with the general principles and other provisions of Community law.

Public security, plurality of the media and prudential rules shall be regarded as legitimate interests within the meaning of the first subparagraph.

Any other public interest must be communicated to the Commission by the Member State concerned and shall be recognized by the Commission after an assessment of its compatibility with the general principles and other provisions of Community law before the measures referred to above may be taken. The Commission shall inform the Member State concerned of its decision within one month of that communication.

Article 22

Application of the Regulation

1. This Regulation alone shall apply to concentrations as defined in Article 3.

2. Regulations No. 17, (EEC) No. 1017/68, (EEC) No. 4056/86 and (EEC) No. 3975/87 shall not apply to concentrations as defined in Article 3.

3. If the Commission finds, at the request of a Member State, that a concentration as defined in Article 3 that has no Community dimension within the meaning of Article 1 creates or strengthens a dominant position as a result of which effective competition would be significantly impeded within the territory of the Member State concerned it may, insofar as the concentration affects trade between Member States, adopt the decisions provided for in Article 8(2), second subparagraph, (3) and (4).

4. Articles 2(1)(a) and (b), 5, 6, 8 and 10 to 20 shall apply. The period within which the proceedings defined in Article 10(1) may be initiated shall begin on the date of the receipt of the request from the Member State. The request must be made within one month at most of the date on which the concentration was made known to the Member State or effected. This period shall begin on the date of the first of those events.

5. Pursuant to paragraph 3 the Commission shall take only the measures strictly necessary to maintain or restore effective competition within the territory of the Member State at the request of which it intervenes.

6. Paragraphs 3 to 5 shall continue to apply until the thresholds referred to in Article 1(2) have been reviewed.

Article 23

Implementing provisions

The Commission shall have the power to adopt implementing provisions concerning the form, content and other details of notifications pursuant to Article 4, time limits pursuant to Article 10, and hearings pursuant to Article 18.

Article 24

Relations with non-member countries

1. The Member States shall inform the Commission of any general difficulties encountered by their undertakings with concentrations as defined in Article 3 in a non-member country.

2. Initially not more than one year after entry into force of this Regulation and thereafter periodically the Commission shall draw up a report examining the treatment accorded to Community undertakings, in the terms referred to in paragraphs 3 and 4, as regards concentrations in non-member countries. The Commission shall submit those reports to the Council, together with any recommendations.

3. Whenever it appears to the Commission, either on the basis of the reports referred to in paragraph 2 or on the basis of other information, that a non-member country does not grant Community undertakings treatment comparable to that granted by the Community to undertakings from that non-member country, the Commission may submit proposals to the Council for the appropriate mandate for negotiation with a view to obtaining comparable treatment for Community undertakings.

4. Measures taken pursuant to this Article shall comply with the obligations of the Community or of the Member States, without prejudice to Article 234 of the Treaty, under international agreements, whether bilateral or multilateral.

Article 25

Entry into force

1. This Regulation shall enter into force on 21 September 1990.

2. This Regulation shall not apply to any concentration which was

the subject of an agreement or announcement or where control was acquired within the meaning of Article 4(1) before the date of this Regulation's entry into force and it shall not in any circumstances apply to any concentration in respect of which proceedings were initiated before that date by a Member State's authority with responsibility for competition.

This Regulation shall be binding in its entirety and directly applicable in all Member States.

Done at Brussels, 21 December 1989.

For the Council
The President
E. Cresson